OVERSIZE

ACPL ITEM
DISCARDED

JEWELRY MAKING AS A HOBBY

JEWELRY MAKING AS A HOBBY

An Illustrated Guide for the Beginner

Robert Wald

Line drawings by Andre Ecuyer

ASSOCIATION PRESS / **New York**

JEWELRY MAKING AS A HOBBY

Copyright © 1972 by Robert Wald

Association Press, 291 Broadway, New York, N.Y. 10007

All rights reserved. No part of this publication may be reprinted, reproduced, transmitted, stored in a retrieval system, or otherwise utilized, in any form or by any means, electronic or mechanical, including photocopying or recording, now existing or hereinafter invented, without the prior written permission of the publisher.

International Standard Book Number: 0-8096-1837-0
Library of Congress Catalog Card Number: 72-8944

Library of Congress Cataloging in Publication Data

Wald, Robert.
  Jewelry making as a hobby.

  1. Jewelry making—Amateurs' manuals.
I. Title.
TS741.W34   739.27   72-8944
ISBN 0-8096-1837-0

Printed in the United States of America

1756117

I dedicate this book to my dear wife and children who left me free to enjoy my hobby and who gave me gifts of metalworking tools I broadly hinted I would like to have on such occasions as Hanukkah, Christmas, Birthday, Father's Day and Wedding Anniversary.

TO THE BEGINNER

Welcome, you who want to work with metal to create jewelry, welcome to a very ancient, highly respected and wonderfully exciting field. From the earliest times, people have sought to enhance their appearance with objects that caught the eye and appealed to their sense of beauty. Among these people were always those with the desire to satisfy the great craving for articles of personal adornment. These were the earliest jewelry craftsmen. And, if you have any idea at all as to what is involved in shaping, joining, texturing, smoothing, and polishing metal to make an item of jewelry, you cannot help but be astounded and fascinated by the handiwork achieved by these artisans in every period of history—with copper, brass, bronze, iron, silver, and gold, and using the simplest of tools and equipment.

The complete story of jewelry making would take many volumes to relate. Such a story could not be limited to the magnificent creations of the Etruscan, Greek, and Roman metalsmiths, the goldsmiths of the Renaissance, or even the pre-Victorian and Victorian craftsmen, without doing a grave injustice to the equally superb workmanship of the jewelry makers among the Aztecs, Mayas and Incas of South America, the Moors in Spain, the diverse tribes in Africa, and the artisans of China, India, Japan, Thailand and other Eastern countries.

The universal appeal of jewelry remains unabated today and will, in all probability, continue as long as human beings inhabit the earth. Is there anyone—man, woman or child—who does not own and wear, if only on special occasions, at least one jewelry trinket? Excepting, of course, those very few who will not wear any jewelry for religious or other personal reasons. Today, much of this appetite for objects of personal adornment is being satisfied by commercial manufacturers who use mass production techniques. There are still, however, thousands of individuals who continue to produce exquisite jewelry through the creativity of their minds and the ingenuity of their hands. Almost daily, more and more novices are becoming intrigued with the jewelry-making processes. Which leads us to the question: "Why not you, too?"

This book has two objectives. One is to interest you in jewelry making as a stimulating and rewarding hobby—for some people perhaps a lifetime career. The other objective is to provide enough of the elementary knowledge and skills necessary to get you started in the right direction. The book was written in the belief that there are many people who have talents and creative abilities that remain unrevealed mainly because they are never searched for and tested. This text is, therefore, aimed at all who are willing to probe the unknown and unexplored *within themselves* in an effort to uncover the riches that exist there. It is also written for those who enjoy working with their hands; who derive great pleasure from taking shapeless objects and giving them form. On the other hand, this book is not intended for professional craftsmen, except as they may wish to use it with such student apprentices as they may have. Nor is it addressed to the hobbyists who have devoted so many hours to mastering the craft that the projects herein offer no challenge to their capabilities.

The book does not cover every aspect of jewelry making by any means, but it does try to illustrate and explain the principal techniques. And, finally, the book is definitely not intended to show off the author's work as a jewelry craftsman.

Every article demonstrated in the projects has been especially designed on the basis of what you, as a newcomer to the craft, can successfully accomplish, working alone or as a student in an introductory art-metal and jewelry-making class.

Use this book as an informal textbook. Each chapter builds to the one which follows in terms of the skills you must acquire in order to become seriously engaged in jewelry making. The same remark applies to the projects which, for the most part, become increasingly difficult as you go from one to the next.

The over-all goal of this book is to make sure that you will not be content merely to copy the jewelry illustrated, but that—once you have the know-how—you will go on to experiment with and design your own creations. The fundamental thing is *to try, to explore, to do.* Only by trying, exploring and doing will you develop the skill, assurance and imagination that can lead you eventually to the mastery of the craft.

A list of companies happy to sell craft metals, tools, equipment, and supplies for the handicrafting of jewelry appears in the Appendix. These concerns offer catalogs and price lists—some free, some for a nominal charge which is usually deductible from your first order. Most of the catalogs provide a tremendous amount of information which is an education in itself.

The author wishes to express his special thanks to the Allcraft Tool and Supply Company and the William Dixon Company for the illustrations of tools, equipment, and jewelry-making supplies they graciously provided for this book.

CONTENTS

To the Beginner   7

1. *Meet The Materials*   15

    The Craft Metals, 15
    How To Buy Craft Metals, 19
    Solder, 22
    Flux, 24
    Jewelry Findings, 24
    Gemstones, 29

2. *Getting Started*   31

    A Place to Work, 31
    Tools and Supplies, 32

3. *Mastering Basic Techniques*   51

    Transferring Designs to Metal, 51
    Drilling Craft Metals, 52
    Cutting Craft Metals, 53
    Filing Metals, 58
    Chasing Metals, 60
    Dapping Metals, 63
    Annealing Metals, 65
    Pickling Metals, 66
    Soldering Metals, 66
    Smoothing Metals, 71
    Polishing and Coloring Metals, 72

CONTENTS

4. *Bracelets* — 75

- PROJECT 1: Copper Open-End Bracelet, 75
- PROJECT 2: Brass/Copper Open-End Bracelet, 78
- PROJECT 3: Sterling Silver Open-End Bracelet, 80
- PROJECT 4: Copper/Silver Bangle Bracelet, 82
- PROJECT 5.: Brass/Silver Bangle Bracelet, 83

5. *Earrings* — 85

- PROJECT 6: Brass/Copper Button Earrings, 85
- PROJECT 7: Copper/Brass Drop Earrings, 87
- PROJECT 8: Silver Button Earrings I, 89
- PROJECT 9: Silver Drop Earrings with Gemstones, 90
- PROJECT 10: Silver Button Earrings II, 92

6. *Cuff Links with Matching Tie Ornaments* — 95

- PROJECT 11: Copper/Brass Cuff Links and Tie Bar, 95
- PROJECT 12: Silver Cuff Links and Tie Bar, 97
- PROJECT 13: Silver Cuff Links and Tie Tack with Gemstones, 97

7. *Rings* — 99

- PROJECT 14: Lady's Brass/Copper Ring, 99
- PROJECT 15: Man's Silver Ring, 101
- PROJECT 16: Lady's Silver Ring with Gemstone, 102

8. *Pins and Brooches* — 105

- PROJECT 17: Copper/Brass Pin, 105
- PROJECT 18: Silver Pin, 108

9. *Chain Making* — 109

- PROJECT 19: Round Link Chain, 109
- PROJECT 20: Handmade Chain, 110
- PROJECT 21: Handmade Chain, with Variations, 111

10. *Pendants* — 113

- PROJECT 22: Brass Heart Pendant, 113
- PROJECT 23: Brass Pendant with Gemstone, 114
- PROJECT 24: Silver Pendant, 116

CONTENTS

11. *Designing Jewelry*   117

   Appendix A. Suppliers   119

   Appendix B. Other Tools and Equipment   121

   Index   123

JEWELRY MAKING AS A HOBBY

1/MEET THE MATERIALS

The Craft Metals

The metals most commonly used in creating jewelry are copper, brass, gilding metal, nickel silver, pure and sterling silver, pure and karat golds, and platinum. The first four metals are called "base" metals mainly to distinguish them from the rarer, more costly silver, gold, and platinum. In the past, craftsmen have used iron, pewter, bronze, aluminum, and even steel in fashioning personal ornaments. Lately, some have added stainless steel to the list. These metals, although still used, are the exception rather than the rule so far as making jewelry is concerned. Before discussing the main qualities of the metals we are interested in, let us define a few terms that are used in describing a metal's characteristics.

Alloy. A *mixture* of two or more metals produced by heating them until they melt, stirring them together, then allowing them to cool and harden. Metals are alloyed because the process changes the basic nature of the metals that are mixed. For example, pure silver is quite soft; whereas alloying it with a small amount of copper hardens it. Also, the melting point of pure silver is 1761 degrees Fahrenheit; that of copper is 1981 degrees. (*Note:* From this point on, all temperatures referred to are in degrees Fahrenheit.) Mixing more and more copper with the silver produces alloys which all have a melting point *lower* than either of the parent metals—one as low as 1135 degrees. This is a remarkable phenomenon of nature and is of great importance to metal workers, as you will learn when we discuss solders and soldering.

Malleable and *malleability.* The ease with which a metal can be hammered, pounded or pressed into various shapes without cracking or returning to its original shape.

Ductile or *ductility*. This refers primarily to the ease with which the metal can be pulled, stretched or drawn (reduction of its diameter, for example, in the case of wire) without breaking.

Oxidation. Some craft metals unite with certain chemicals in the air—e.g., sulfur—to form an oxide which usually changes the color of the metal's surface. The oxidizing process occurs more rapidly when these metals are heated. There are times, you will find, when you do not want a metal to oxidize or tarnish, as most people refer to it. There are other times when you do want it to happen so as to color, or "antique," a piece of jewelry you have made (more about this later).

Now we turn to the metals themselves. As noted on the previous page, these are the principal metals used by craftsmen in making jewelry.

COPPER

This metal, with its appealing red color, has been used by man for at least eight thousand years for all kinds of articles, including jewelry. Copper is soft, very malleable and ductile and rather inexpensive, which makes it a fine material for beginners to work with. One of its great disadvantages, however, is that it oxidizes rather quickly unless it is protected with a coat of colorless metal lacquer.

BRASS

Brass is an alloy of copper and zinc. Various brass alloys are manufactured for different purposes by changing the proportion of copper to zinc. The yellow brass in our jewelry projects is a mixture of about 65 per cent copper to about 35 per cent zinc. Brass is a little less malleable and ductile than copper, but this presents no problem for jewelry making. Its cost is slightly higher than copper, and, though it does not tarnish as readily as copper, it does require a coating of lacquer to forestall oxidation.

GILDING METAL

This is a form of brass, an alloy that varies between 80 per cent copper to 20 per cent zinc and 95 per cent copper with 5 per cent zinc. Because its color is very close to that of gold, gilding metal is sometimes used to imitate that metal. Other than that, its qualities are very similar to yellow brass. Gilding metal is also known by other names such as Nu-Gold, Dixgold, tombac and pinchbeck, depending on who sells it and where it is made.

NICKEL SILVER

This metal, often called German silver, is an alloy of nickel, copper and zinc. Its color closely resembles that of silver, which accounts for its name, even though it contains no silver at all. Much less subject to oxidization than copper or brass, it is also less malleable and ductile than these metals. In fact, it is tough and quite springy, which makes it very useful for fastening devices such as pins for brooches.

MEET THE MATERIALS

SILVER

Pure, or fine, silver (it is referred to both ways) is almost perfectly white and next to pure gold is the most malleable and ductile metal in the world. One use (there are others) is as a setting for certain shapes of gemstones. It can be polished to a beautiful, sparkling luster and is very resistant to oxidation. Being a precious metal, naturally the cost of fine silver is higher than the price of any of the base metals. Pure silver is too soft, however, for most jewelry projects, since it bends and dents too easily. To overcome this disadvantage, pure silver is often alloyed with copper to harden it.

Sterling Silver. This is an alloy of 92½ per cent pure silver and 7½ per cent copper. It is the form of silver as well as *the metal* most widely used commercially and by handicraftsmen not only for jewelry but for what is generally called flatware—spoons, forks, knives (handles only), candy and serving dishes, bowls, and many other articles. While tougher than pure silver, sterling silver remains ductile and malleable enough that the craftsman can do wonders with it in creating designs of the greatest complexity and delicacy. Its one major disadvantage is that the copper in the alloy makes it subject to oxidation. But because of sterling silver's many other outstanding characteristics, most craftsmen, and the public as a whole, are willing to overlook this minor disadvantage.

Coin Silver, Mexican Silver, American Indian Silver. These alloys are essentially the same. Each basically contains 90 per cent pure silver with 10 per cent copper. Up until 1966, U.S. dimes, quarters and half dollars were made of this harder, more durable alloy, hence the name *coin silver.* Certain groups of craftsmen—Mexicans (particularly those living near the U.S. border), American Indians and others—used this alloy. Its lower silver content made it less expensive than sterling and, also, silver coins were readily available to be melted down and formed into sheets and wire from which jewelry could be made that would sell for much more than the value of the coins. A few craft metal suppliers sell coin silver to craftsmen who like the decorative effects that can be achieved more easily with this alloy than with sterling silver.

GOLD

Pure, or fine, gold (both terms are used) is naturally yellow in color and is the most malleable and ductile of all metals. It can be hammered and rolled into sheets thinner than the thinnest paper you have ever seen, and a pea-sized bit of it can be drawn into a wire over thirty-three miles long. Gold, in all its forms, is many times more expensive than silver. Fine gold does not oxidize. Like fine silver, it is too soft to be used, except as a setting for certain shapes of gemstones and a few other special purposes. Pure gold is alloyed with other metals for three principal reasons: (1) to make it harder and more resistant to wear; (2) to reduce its cost; and (3) to obtain different colors. All gold alloys are considered in terms of karats (abbreviated to K) of gold. The term karat (not to be confused with "carat" which is a measure of the weight/size of the more valuable gemstones) is a measure of the amount of pure gold in the alloy. Thus—

24K gold is pure, or fine, gold;

18K gold is 18 parts fine gold, 6 parts other metals;
14K gold is 14 parts fine gold, 10 parts other metals;
10K gold is 10 parts fine gold, 14 parts other metals.
There are other karats of gold, but 18K and particularly 14K are the most popular.

Gold is sold in four main colors. Other metals mixed with fine gold increase its durability. Different colors are obtained as follows:

yellow. Silver, copper, zinc. This is the most widely used color for jewelry making and at the same karat level it is generally easier to work with than the others. For example, 14K yellow gold is more malleable and ductile than 14K white gold.

green. More silver and less copper than yellow gold. This color is mostly used for the reproduction of certain antique-style jewelry.

red/pink. More copper, less silver than yellow gold. This color is often used in combination with yellow gold for a contrasting effect.

white. Nickel, copper, and zinc. White gold, which is brittle and hard to work with, is usually used with diamonds, since its color blends well with these gems.

PLATINUM

This metal, the most costly of all the craft metals, does not tarnish and is highly ductile and malleable. Its gray-white color harmonizes beautifully with diamonds and, since it is much stronger than white gold, it is much preferred to that metal as the setting for jewelry containing many diamonds or the more valuable diamonds. Its cost, unfortunately, puts it out of the reach of most individual jewelry craftsmen.

You will find these metals offered in the catalogs of craft metal suppliers, and it is well for you to know something about their main characteristics. The projects in this book, however, will involve only copper, brass, and sterling silver plus a little pure silver for the setting of a few gemstones. These three metals have been chosen for the following reasons:

1. Being fairly inexpensive, copper and brass are good metals on which to practice, also, very attractive articles of jewelry can be fashioned from them as has been for thousands of years. Sterling silver (which we will refer to simply as silver in following pages) has its own special qualities, and a well-designed, well-made piece of silver jewelry often becomes a family heirloom handed down from generation to generation.

2. Copper, brass, and silver get along well with each other when paired together in such combinations as copper-brass, copper-silver, brass-silver. Further, through the use of the three metals—whether in combination or alone—you experience the "feel" of each metal, and how each one differs from the others even in small ways. As a result, you will learn to expect individual differences in other metals—gold, for example—should you decide one day to create something in that metal.

MEET THE MATERIALS

3. Finally, these metals were chosen because—with the exception of gold and platinum—they are offered in a greater variety of shapes and sizes than are any other of the craft metals.

How to Buy Craft Metals

The suppliers of craft metals are listed in the Appendix. These metals are sold in the form of a flat sheet or as wire in various thicknesses or gauges. The Brown and Sharpe (abbreviated B&S) gauging system is commonly used in the United States for measuring the thickness of nonferrous metals (those that are not iron or an iron alloy, such as steel). The B&S gauge, shown in Fig. 1, is commonly used for determining the thickness of the sheet and wire forms of the craft and other nonferrous metals. One side of the gauge shows the thickness as a whole number; the other side in thousandths of an inch. You may use either dimension in ordering craft metals. The gauge of a metal is found by inserting the sheet or wire into the smallest *slot* (not the hole) that will accept it and reading the number opposite the slot.

FIGURE 1

Fig. 2 illustrates the approximate thickness of sheet metal along with the B&S gauge number which corresponds to the thickness. Notice that the smaller the whole gauge number the thicker the metal (the decimal numbers are, of course, just the reverse).

All craft metals are sold by weight—the base metals in the well-known avoirdupois ounces and pounds of the kitchen or the butcher's scale; the precious metals in troy pennyweights, ounces and pounds. Since dealers' catalogs usually show troy weights in relation to the precious metals they sell, you should have some idea of what constitutes this weight system:

SHEET STERLING SILVER

Available in the following size blanks:

6" x 12"	2" x 3"
6" x 6"	1" x 3"
3" x 6"	1" x 6"
2" x 6"	3" x 3"

In the gauges listed

THICKNESS B&S Gauge		Weight per sq. inch troy ounces
14	for heavy rings and bracelets, holloware	.351
16	for average rings, holloware	.278
18	for lightweight pierced designs, holloware	.221
18	} for brooches, earrings, beads, buttons, and bezels for settings, etc.	.221
20		.175
22		.139
24		.110
26		.087

FIGURE 2

---

24 grains	=	1 pennyweight (dwt)
20 pennyweights (dwts)	=	1 ounce
12 ounces	=	1 pound

(*Note:* The troy ounce is about 10 per cent heavier than the avoirdupois ounce.)

Lest this unfamiliar weight system confuse you, you should know that though these suppliers do base their precious metal prices on the troy weight of the pieces you purchase, their catalogs or price lists generally indicate the cost of the metals in terms of the dimensions of the items you may wish to buy. In ordering metals you should provide the supplier with the following information:

1. Sheet metal—the kind of metal, the linear dimensions (*e.g.,* 12 in. x 12 in., 6 in. x 6 in., etc.), and the *gauge.* Sheet copper and brass in each available gauge is usually sold by the square foot. Smaller sizes are sold by the piece, as will be dealt with shortly. Fine or sterling silver, being more expensive, can be bought in each available gauge, starting in some cases with a piece as small as 2 in. x 1 in. x 28 ga. The same applies to gold.

2. Circles—the kind of metal, the diameter and the gauge. Dealers' catalogs indicate the sizes and gauges they offer.

3. Wire—the kind of metal, the quantity, the gauge and shape. Depending on the supplier, copper and brass wire is sold either by a preset number of feet (5 ft., 10 ft., 25 ft., 50 ft.), by the spool (4 oz. and 1 lb. as a rule), and by the coil (1 lb.) in a limited number of gauges and in only one shape—round. The number of feet on a spool or coil decreases as the gauge of the wire increases, because a foot of 14-ga. wire, for example, is thicker and weighs more than a foot of 20-ga. wire. Fine and sterling silver wire comes in many shapes (Fig. 3). In ordering the flat wire (also termed oblong or rectangular wire) you must designate two gauges—the gauge of the width *and* the thickness (*e.g.,* 8 ga. wide x 16 ga. thick).

A brief word needs to be said about bezels (see Fig. 4). In jewelry crafting, a bezel is primarily a rectangular wire, called bezel wire, which you shape closely around a gemstone so as to secure the stone to an article of jewelry. There are two types of bezel wire: plain and

MEET THE MATERIALS

STERLING SILVER WIRE (STOCK SIZES)
Approximate Length —Per Troy Ounce

Nearest Fractional Size	Fig. 417-2 ROUND		Fig. 417-3 HALF ROUND		Fig. 417-4 SQUARE		Fig. 417-5 RECTANGULAR	
	B&S Gauge	Feet	B&S Gauge	Feet	B&S Gauge	Feet	B&S Gauge	Feet
5/16"			5/16" base	5 Inches				
5/32"			6 "	1½				
1/8"	8	1¼	8 "	2½	8	1		
	10	2	10 "	3¾				
5/64"	12	3			12	2¼		
1/16"	14	4¾	14 "	9½	14	3¾		
	16	7½			16	6	4 x 16	1½
	18	12			18	9¼	6 x 18	2¼
1/32"	20	19						
	22	30					8 x 22	4¾
1/64"							*8 x 26	7½

* Fine Silver only

FIGURE 3

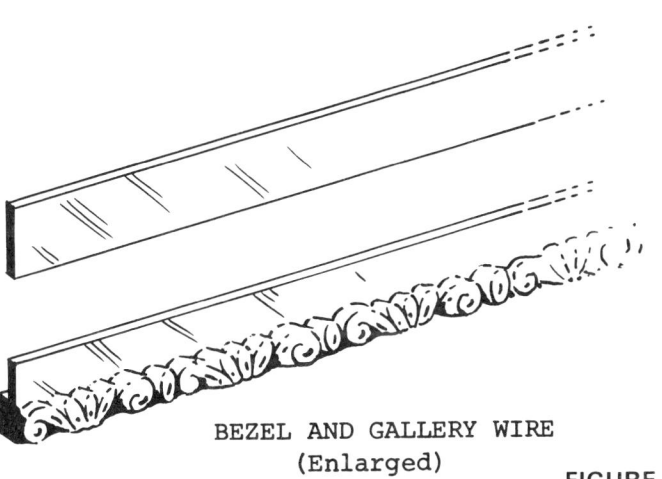

BEZEL AND GALLERY WIRE
(Enlarged)

FIGURE 4

decorated. The plain wire is obtainable in both pure and sterling silver. The pure silver is the better choice because its softness makes it easy to shape and to fit firmly around the stone. The standard size is 8 ga. x 16 ga. or ⅛ in. x 16 ga., which are almost identical dimensions. The decorated type of bezel wire—more frequently called gallery wire—has a design stamped along the lower part of one of its wider surfaces. On the opposite surface is a sort of "ledge" on which the gemstone rests. Gallery wire is made only in sterling silver and is not recommended for the novice craftsman. Plain bezel wire 8 ga. x 30 ga. is offered in pure yellow gold and in 14K and 18K yellow gold. The pure metal is preferable for its softness.

In purchasing materials, you will note that the greater the amount you order—the precious metals especially—the lower the cost per square inch, square foot, or running foot. As a beginning craftsman, you are probably better off paying the somewhat higher prices for the smaller quantities than investing large sums in materials you may not use for a long time. Some suppliers offer sheet copper and sterling silver in a variety of small-sized forms: squares, rectangles, diamonds, ovals, and in such special shapes as hearts, trees, leaves, religious crosses, blanks for rings, animal forms and many others. These are sold by the piece, and you pay extra for the work done in preparing these shapes. The vast majority of craftsmen design, draw and cut their own forms and shapes, however, and—since this book is largely based on the "learn by doing" philosophy of teaching—you are urged to do likewise.

Solder

A solder is a metal alloy used to join metal parts together by heating the solder until it melts and flows between the parts to be united. The place at which the union is made is usually referred to as a join or joint. The heating and joining process is called soldering. There are two main types of solder:

Soft solders. These are usually alloys of tin and lead in different proportions that are primarily used with the base metals. Craftsmen avoid the use of soft solder with their silver and gold jewelry except to join certain accessories to the articles. One big disadvantage of soft solders is that their grayish-white color stands out glaringly against metals of another color such as copper and brass. Another drawback is that the join made with them is not too strong. However, since soft solder does have a function in certain jewelry-making projects due to its low melting point, you should have some on hand. The more common tin and lead alloys and their melting points are:

```
50% tin to 50% lead . . . . . . 450 degrees
60% tin to 40% lead . . . . . . 395 degrees
63% tin to 37% lead . . . . . . 356 degrees
```

These solders are generally referred to as 50/50, 60/40, and 63/37. Soft solders are available in a variety of forms. Some suppliers offer a silver-colored soft solder in thin wire form that contains no lead, does not tarnish and melts at 350 degrees. This solder or a 1/16 in. diameter 60/40 solid wire soft solder is fine for your purposes. The first can be bought in short lengths, the second as a coiled spool. Because a small amount will go a long way, you should buy the smallest available quantity of either of the recommended types.

Hard solders. Any solder with a melting point higher than 1000 degrees is considered a hard solder. Most of the soldering of precious-metal jewelry parts is done with hard solders because they make a much stronger join than any of the soft solders. Hard solders are also alloys, and there are different ones for silver, gold and platinum. Hard silver solders—which are alloys of silver, copper and zinc—are made in three principal grades: Easy, Medium and

MEET THE MATERIALS

Hard. These grades are based on the melting points of the alloy, and the higher the melting point the greater the skill required to perform the soldering operation. Thus the Easy grade requires only a fair amount of skill, the Medium grade a greater amount, and the Hard grade requires the greatest amount because its melting point approaches the melting point of the silver parts being joined. The hard silver solders and their melting points are:

Easy	.1325 degrees
Medium	.1390 degrees
Hard	.1425 degrees

There are grades of hard silver solder which melt at 1450 degrees and 1460 degrees (generally termed the IT grade), but these are used for special purposes not covered in this book. There are also grades called Extra Easy or Easy Flo which have melting points below 1325 degrees. These have a yellowish color which shows up against silver. These grades, therefore, are used only in places where the solder will not be seen, such as the back of a pin or earring. Hard solders for gold and platinum are made in the same grades as for silver. In addition, the gold solders are alloyed to match the color karat of the gold parts being soldered—*i.e.,* there are Easy, Medium and Hard 14K and 18K yellow gold solders for joining, respectively, 14K and 18K yellow gold parts.

There is a good reason for the existence of the various grades of hard solder. Some articles of jewelry may need two, three, four or even more soldering operations in their construction. If only one grade of solder is used, there is always the danger that the heat required to perform the later soldering operations will cause the solder of the earlier operations to melt, resulting in the opening up of joints and the falling apart of pieces previously soldered together. Let us assume a jewelry article calls for six soldering operations. Using Hard-grade solder (the highest melting point) in the first two operations, Medium grade in the next two and Easy grade in the last two can substantially reduce, or even eliminate entirely, the risk of any parts becoming unsoldered.

Hard solder is sold in various forms: strip, sheet, wire and clipped (1/16 in. squares). For the projects in this book you will need a ¼-oz. sheet of Easy-, Medium- and Hard-grade silver solder. The length and width of the sheet may vary a little from one supplier to another, and the thickness may be either 26 or 30 gauge. The dimensions do not matter, but the thinner gauge is preferable because it is easier to cut into small squares, the form in which you will be using the hard solders.

Before leaving the solders it is worth noting that hard silver solder is often used to join base metal parts when stronger bonds than those provided by the soft solders are desired. The problem is that the white color of the silver solder does not blend with the colors of copper and brass. There is a brass solder, however, whose melting point is quite high (1530 degrees) but still within the capability of the beginning craftsman. You may wish to have a 1-oz. sheet of this on hand.

Flux

Earlier it was said that certain craft metals oxidize quite rapidly when heated. When joining metal parts, however, they and the solder used must be heated to the melting point of that solder if the parts are to be united. Unless something else is added to the soldering process, the oxides produced by the heat build a kind of "chemical wall" that prevents the solder from flowing out to unite the parts. That something else is a substance called "flux." There are different fluxes for soft- and hard-soldering operations:

Soft soldering flux. Two forms are available: paste and liquid. In jewelry making the liquid form usually is to be preferred. A 2-ox. bottle or jar will last for a long time.

Hard soldering flux. This, too, is available in two forms: white paste and liquid. Although the liquid flux has an advantage over the paste in that it does not boil so readily when heat is applied, the paste is to be preferred for reasons explained later when "how to solder" is explored. A 1-oz. jar, sold under the trade name of Handy Flux, will cover as many soldering operations as you will do in a year or more.

Jewelry Findings

In jewelry making the word "finding" is used to describe any accessory (device) that is soldered or is otherwise fixed to a piece of jewelry to enable the wearer to fasten the jewelry somewhere on his or her person. There are many different kinds of findings available to the craftsmen. Some professionals prefer to make some of their own findings, often incorporating these into the design of their jewelry. You yourself will do that in several of the projects herein. There are certain findings, however, that require very special skills and tools to fabricate, and it is better to purchase these.

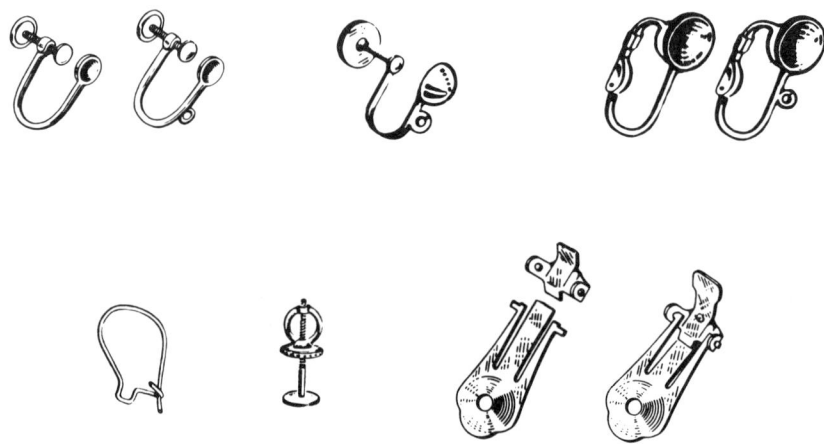

FIGURE 5

MEET THE MATERIALS

FINDINGS FOR EARRINGS

Ear Wires (also called screwbacks). These have a threaded wire which is turned to fasten an earring to an ear lobe.

Ear Clips. These have springs that exert pressure to hold the earring on the ear.

Ear Findings for Pierced Ears. These, of course, are for women with pierced ear lobes. A variety of styles are available, two of which are illustrated. (See Fig. 5.)

You will find that some earring findings are plain; others are equipped with a half ball (dome) or full ball as ornamentation. The plain ones have a small cup which serves as a receptacle for the solder needed to attach the finding to whatever metal ornament the craftsman creates. Soft solder is quite often used, since the heat required for hard soldering can melt the delicate accessory or parts of it can become unsoldered. One exception to this is a style of ear clip which comes in two sections—one, called a joint, to be hard-soldered to the ornament, and the other, the spring section, which is fastened in the joint after the soldering is completed. Thus, the high temperature has no opportunity to destroy the elasticity that gives springiness to the metal.

You will also notice that certain earring findings have a peg on which a pearl, drilled halfway through for this purpose, can be cemented. Among all the styles are some that have a small ring either built in or soldered onto the finding. These are for what are known as drop, or "dangle," earrings, and the parts that dangle hang from these rings. The style of earring finding to use depends upon the preference of the person who will be wearing the earrings. Some women prefer screwbacks, others clips, and those with pierced ears usually like to display the fact that they have suffered through the minor surgery required for this type of earring.

FINDINGS FOR CUFF LINKS

The standard types, generally referred to as cuff-link backs, have a section which swivels on a sort of double stem. The swivel section contains a spring which holds the part in a vertical position for inserting it into the shirt cuff's buttonholes; then, when turned, it is held in a horizontal position to keep the cuff link in place. This spring, like all springs, also loses its elasticity under high temperatures. Therefore cuff-link backs are made for hard or soft soldering or both. The "both" kind works well for all, provided that great care is taken when used

FIGURE 6

with hard solder. The soft-soldering type has a cup much like those of some earring findings and for the same purpose. Since anything, such as cuff links, worn on the arm is exposed to many more mechanical blows than, for example, earrings, the hard solder is preferable. And the style that comes with a separate swivel section, joint and rivet is the safest for a beginning craftsman to use. (See Fig. 6.) The joint is hard-soldered to the ornament, after which the two sections are united with the rivet.

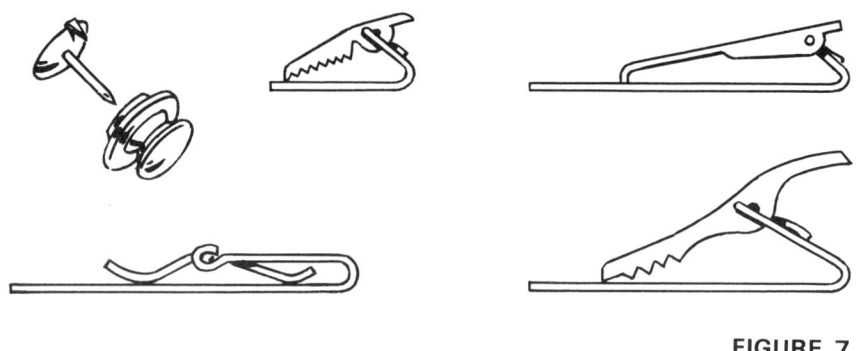

FIGURE 7

FINDINGS FOR TIE JEWELRY

Tie clips. These have teeth-like notches and a spring to hold the jewelry on the tie. Those with many notches are often called alligator tie clips because of their resemblance to the alligator's lower jaw. The presence of the spring makes these suitable only for soft soldering.

Tie tacks. These consist of a post and clutch back which grips the post to hold the jewelry on the tie. In one style the clutch back is attached to a chain which, in turn, is attached to a bar. The bar is to be slipped into a buttonhole on the shirtfront so that the tie can swing more freely than with the plain style which is usually worn pinned through the shirtfront and tie. The posts come plain or with a peg on which to cement a half-drilled pearl, or with a small disk on one end. On some, the disk has a tiny metal point that, by slightly piercing the tie, prevents an ornament from turning when it is being worn. Some tie ornaments are designed to be worn only in one position and may look quite odd if turned from that position (a human head or a person's initials, for example). The plain posts are used with hard solder; those with disks are used with either soft or hard solder. The problem with both styles is that excessive heat can soften the metal post to such a degree that it will easily bend out of shape. How to guard against this will be taken up later in our tie jewelry projects.

Tie bars or slides. These can be bought, of course, but you will be shown how to construct your own. Ornaments can be hard-soldered to them providing the heat is applied as carefully as with the tie-back posts. See Fig. 7.

MEET THE MATERIALS

FINDINGS FOR BROOCHES OR PINS

The standard findings for brooches or pins consist of a joint, a safety catch and a pin stem. (See Fig. 8.) The joints and catches to be joined with silver jewelry are made for either soft or hard soldering; those for gold are only for hard soldering; and those for copper and brass are only for soft soldering. Joints and catches designed for soft soldering have a larger base than do the hard-solder types so that more solder can be applied under the devices since soft solder makes a weaker join. A few catches open at the top; most open at one side. The side-opening catches offer greater security against losing the brooch. The pin stem is not fixed into the joint until all hard-soldering operations on the particular article have been completed, because the heat involved can decrease the hardness and springiness which the pin stem must have if it is to perform its job properly. Pin stems are riveted to the joint, and some can be had with the rivets attached. In the others you supply the rivet (nickel silver and brass wire can be bought for this purpose). The type of pin stem you elect to use is a matter of personal preference.

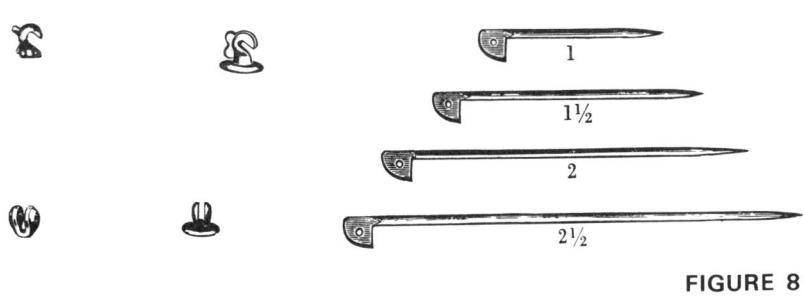

FIGURE 8

The joints, catches and pin stems all come in a variety of sizes. The smaller sizes are used with the smaller brooches; the larger with the larger ones. In a few supply catalogs these findings are matched up so that you can order those that go with one another. Pin stems come in various lengths. It's better to have on hand some that are too long rather than too short because it is easy to cut the pin stem down to length and then file a new point on it. Finally, there's a finding called a pinback which combines the joint, catch and pin stem all in one unit. These are not very desirable inasmuch as they can only be used with soft solder, and with ornaments that completely hide the bar which supports the pinback's parts.

FINDINGS FOR BRACELETS AND NECKLACES

These are principally for the link (flexible) type bracelet or necklace as opposed to those created from solid sheet or wire (see Fig. 9). The link styles generally require a metal ring, such as a jump ring, on one end of the bracelet or necklace and a fastening device on the other end to secure the jewelry on the wearer's arm or neck as the case may be. All the findings listed below come in a number of different sizes.

Jump rings. These are obtainable in round and oval shapes. They are used for purposes other than as part of a fastening device—*e.g.,* as links for chains, for linking charms to a bracelet, to attach the findings listed below to the jewelry, and so on. Later on you will be shown how to make your own jump rings as well as the proper way to employ them.

Sister hooks.   Their curved legs swivel on a round joint so that they can be hooked over a ring.

Spring rings.   These have a thin wire which moves inside a small round tube and presses against a built-in spring. Pulling back on the wire's tiny knob opens the spring ring so that it can be closed over a ring on the other side of the bracelet or necklace.

Fold-over catches or clasps.   These are box-like devices in which the hinged lid folds over a ring and snaps shut to hold the jewelry on the person.

FIGURE 9

These are by no means all the findings available to the jewelry craftsman. Those illustrated and explained, however, are the types most often used, and include a number you will need in creating your own jewelry. Many of the findings, but not all, come in a variety of metals and metal finishes so that you can almost always match the color of the findings to the color of the ornament to which the accessories are to be joined. In regard to silver and gold jewelry, it is standard practice to match the *alloy* of the findings to that of the main jewelry part—*i.e.*, sterling silver ear wires for sterling silver earrings, 14K yellow gold cuff backs for 14K yellow gold cuff links, and so on. Findings are usually obtainable in the following metals or metal finishes:

14K gold (yellow and white)
gold filled (yellow and white)
gold plated (yellow)
sterling silver
nickel
nickel plated
copper plated
brass

Gold-filled metal consists of a core of base metal on which a layer of gold (usually 12K) is welded to one or more of its surfaces. In addition to findings, this metal is also to be had in the form of yellow-gold-filled sheet, square, round and half-round wire. It is principally used by commercial manufacturers of less expensive jewelry because it wears well, and closely resembles solid 14K yellow gold jewelry while costing considerably less. Gold-filled findings may be substituted for the solid gold findings if you wish to economize. A plated metal (yellow gold, nickel, copper, etc.) consists of a base metal on which a thin layer (1/100,000 inch or less) of another metal is electrolytically deposited. Plated findings are quite inexpensive and are only suitable for soft soldering because high temperatures will burn the plating away.

MEET THE MATERIALS

29

Yellow-gold-plated accessories are used only as a substitute for brass; never with solid gold jewelry.

Gemstones

Some of our projects will involve the setting of inexpensive gemstones. A number of excellent books have been written about these materials, and the knowledge you gain from reading the less technical ones can be useful as you progress in jewelry making. For our present purposes, however, the brief information presented here will suffice.

Actually, to many contemporary craftsmen, almost any colorful stone of a suitable size and shape—smoothly polished or not—that appeals to a person's sense of beauty qualifies for use

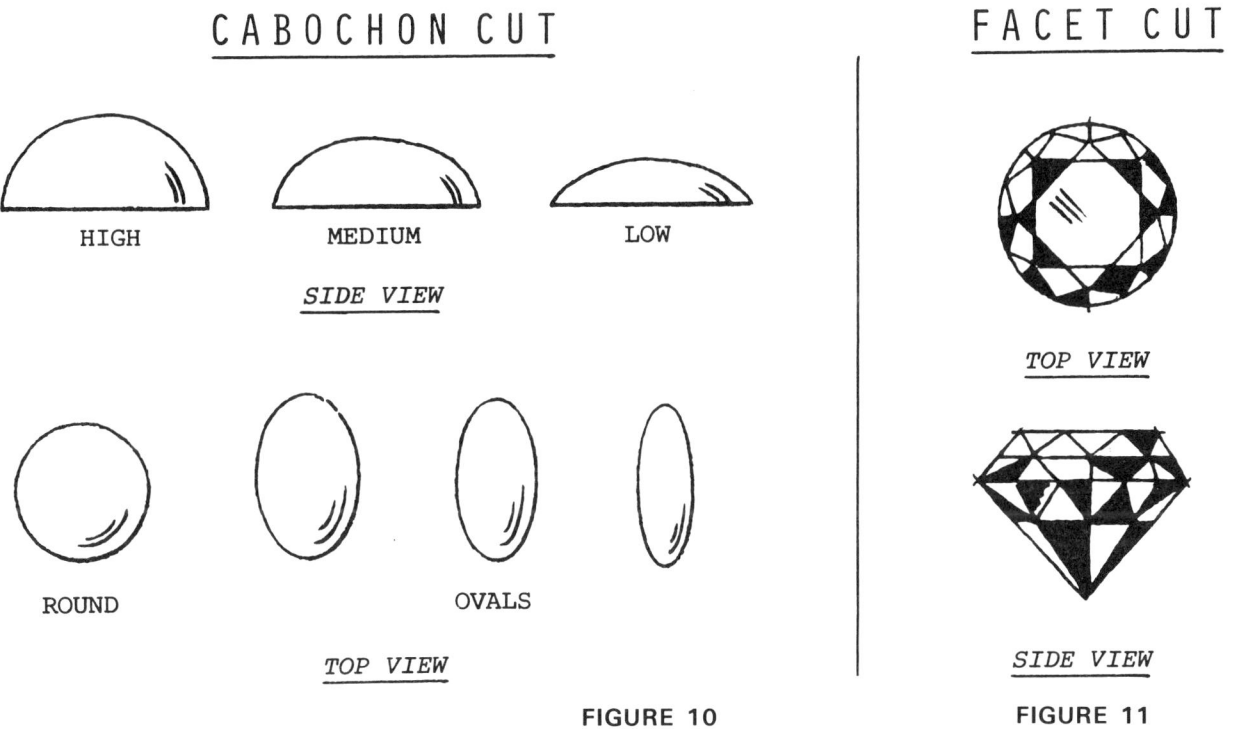

FIGURE 10   FIGURE 11

in jewelry. If you feel this way then do not overlook the smaller, handsome stones that may be found in a backyard or field, along a seashore, or along the banks of many inland bodies of water. Gemstones have long been divided into two main categories: *precious* (*e.g.,* diamond, ruby, sapphire, emerald and some opals) and *semiprecious* (*e.g.,* amethyst, rose quartz, tiger-eye, agate, obsidian, jade, tourmaline, peridot, topaz, and many others). This is a rather artificial division since a well-shaped, superior specimen of true topaz (there is a substitute called citrine or quartz topaz) will have a greater value than an inferior diamond of the same shape and size.

Precious stones, and the more highly prized semiprecious stones, are sold by the carat weight—a carat being equal to a little more than 1/3 dwt. The other semiprecious stones, except tumbled stones (explained below), are sold by their size measured in millimeters. One inch equals about 25½ millimeters (abbreviated mm.), or 1 mm. is roughly .04 or 1/25 inch. Tumbled stones, being the least valued of the semiprecious stones, are sold either by the piece or in bulk form according to the avoirdupois weight of the lot. Gemstones are provided in three primary forms:

Tumbled. These are irregular stones made smooth and polished by tumbling them in a motorized revolving barrel along with, first, successively finer grains of an abrasive such as carborundum, then with various kinds of polishing powders. Basically only the less rare stones are tumbled.

Cabochon (ka-boh-shon'). In this style (see Fig. 10), from a side view, the bottom of the stone is usually cut flat while the top is variously rounded. From a top view, a cabochon-cut stone may be shaped in a round or oval fashion. The rarer opaque semiprecious—as well as the opaque precious (*e.g.,* ruby, precious opal)—are styled or cut cabochon as a rule.

Faceted (fas'-et-ed). In this style (see Fig. 11), the gemstones are cut with a varying number of geometrically arranged surfaces or planes. By and large, only the transparent and translucent precious and rarer semiprecious stones are styled this way to take advantage of the reflective and refractive effect the facets have on the light rays entering the stone.

GETTING STARTED

A Place to Work

A workbench in a space set aside as a workshop along with storage shelves or cabinets, or both, is an ideal setup, but actually one can start anywhere—in a private home, apartment, house trailer or even in a converted barn. All that is needed is a place for storing tools and supplies and a simple workbench or table (even the family's kitchen table) on which to work. A jeweler's workbench can, of course, be purchased. However, publications such as *Popular Mechanics, Family Handyman* and most do-it-yourself books on carpentry, home repairs and woodworking contain plans for the construction of workbenches and tables that almost anyone can assemble with common tools. There are plans for worktables that fold against a wall, fit or fold inside a closet or under a staircase, or into many other tight and unlikely spaces.

If you are relegated to using a household table as your work surface, protect it with a piece of heavy cloth on top of which you have placed a smooth sheet of aluminum (sold in most hardware stores) cut to the size of the tabletop. A piece of 3/8-inch or ½-inch plywood can be substituted if the aluminum is unobtainable. (During soldering operations, the surface of the workbench or table should be safeguarded against the heat and flame of the torch by a 12 x 12 inch pad of ½-inch asbestos millboard or 3/8-inch asbestos transite.)

You should provide a shelf of some kind below the bench top for catching the dust and small scraps of precious metals resulting from sawing, filing and cutting. Use your ingenuity in improvising a tray that will serve the purpose. However you plan the shelf or catch pan, its top surface should be smooth and nonporous so that all the dust and scraps can easily be swept up for storage. Any material such as plain linoleum, formica, flat rectangular-shaped baking tins and the like will work very well. Finally, the tray must be placed in such a way that, when in use, it does not make you uncomfortable during your sawing or filing operations.

After a fairly substantial amount of dust and scraps of silver (also gold and platinum—the base metals do not count) has been accumulated, it can be brought or mailed to a company that refines these metals. The company, in turn, will pay cash or give you a credit toward the purchase of new metal, the amount dependent upon the weight of the metal received and its current market value. Silver dust should be kept in one container, clean scrap pieces in another, and pieces of silver containing solder in a third, for this is the way it must be delivered to the refiners. Also, it is wise to pass a magnet through the dust to pick up any iron particles that may have been worn or chipped off the saw blades or files, as a higher price is paid for clean dust.

You will also need means for storing your tools, equipment and supplies. Such items as cabinets, shelves and drawers can be bought, but most of the publications indicated above will have plans for building these objects as well as illustrations of how to make hangers for files, pliers and practically every tool you will use. Plastic containers, shoe boxes and other cardboard containers, clean food cans and jars and similar receptacles will do to keep small parts in if you have no other alternative. The principal idea is to have a place for everything, and everything in its place. It can be terribly frustrating to have to stop in the middle of the jewelry-making process to hunt frantically for a particular tool or the supply item that you need.

Tools and Supplies

This section introduces the basic tools, equipment and supplies required by a jewelry craftsman. The list is compiled with the belief that it is better for you to know what you need in order to do the required work with a reasonable assurance of satisfaction and success, rather than dishonestly to lead you into believing that jewelry work can be done with about anything that happens to be at hand. However, do not let the length of the listing discourage you. There is no need to buy every item in one fell swoop unless you want to and can afford it. Buy what you can when you can. Meanwhile, occupy yourself by carefully reading this book from cover to cover, and with sending for catalogs to the dealers listed in the Appendix. Study the catalogs as they come in, compare prices, prepare your work place and begin making the substitutes and improvisations that you will find suggested in the list below. Then, before you know it, you will be working on your first piece of jewelry.

Among the most valuable and practical "tools" you can have for forming, bending, twisting, coaxing and cajoling craft metals into the desired shapes are your hands. Not only can they induce the metals to take on the most artistic forms, but they can achieve it without the disfiguring marks that many tools leave behind. Since your hands cannot accomplish every task, however, other aids are needed. In purchasing tools and equipment, it is always sensible to buy first-quality items even though they may cost somewhat more. The better grade tools work more efficiently and effectively and, given good care, last much longer than the inferior grades. Thus in the long run you actually save money. You may already have in your home

GETTING STARTED

some of the implements and materials recorded below; others you will find in certain local stores; all are available from jewelry tool and supply houses. Whenever feasible, suggestions are given for making your own substitutes. Those items that are desirable to have are listed elsewhere; the following are items you absolutely need to get started!

FOR HOLDING METAL

Bench vise with a 2-in. to 3-in. jaw. (See Fig. 12.) One type is bolted down on the work surface; the other is clamped to it. Vise jaws have small teethlike projections which grip objects clamped in the jaws to keep them from shifting. Unless these teeth are padded in some way, ugly scars which are hard to remove will be left on the craft metals and other items held in the vise. Fig. 13 shows the methods by which vise jaws can be covered with shields made of metals or wood (20 ga. or 22 ga. copper, aluminum, etc.).

FIGURE 12

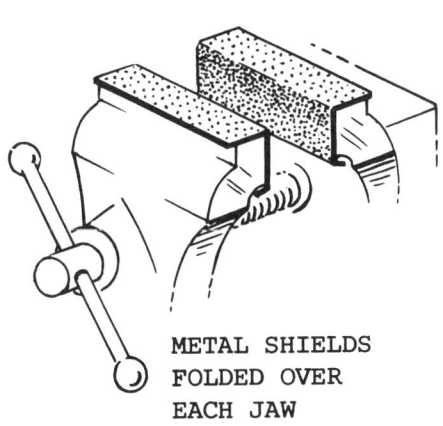

METAL SHIELDS FOLDED OVER EACH JAW

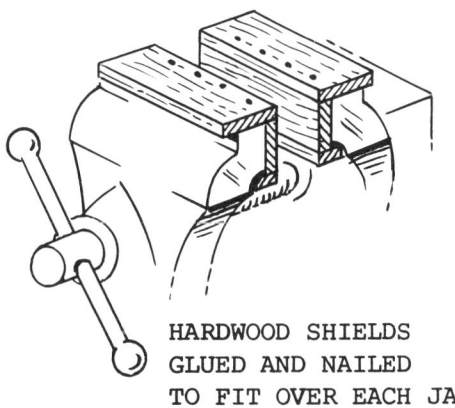

HARDWOOD SHIELDS GLUED AND NAILED TO FIT OVER EACH JAW

FIGURE 13

Bench pin. This is a device, made of wood, on which a piece of craft metal is held during sawing operations with the jeweler's saw. (See Fig. 14.) A V-shaped notch is cut in the pin to permit freedom of movement for the saw blade as it cuts through the metal. One type clamps to the work surface, the second fits in a slot chiseled into the front of the workbench, the third is screwed to this same surface. The tray for catching precious metal scraps and dust is placed below the pin. The type which fastens with a C-clamp is one you should easily be able to make for yourself.

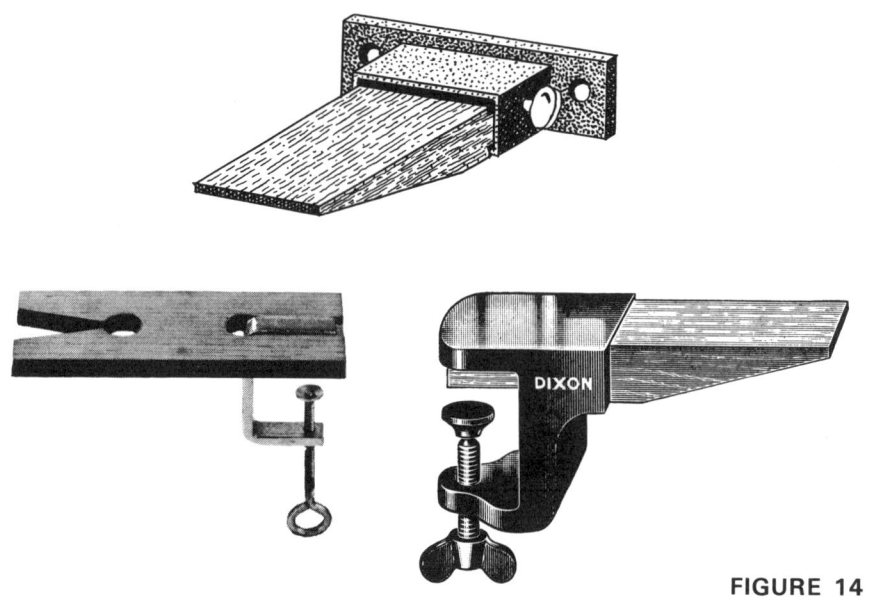

FIGURE 14

Ring clamp. This hand-held device is for holding objects that are to be filed or polished and are too small to be held in the hand or clamped in the bench vise. (See Fig. 15.) The object is placed either in the curved or in the straight end of the clamp with the wooden wedge in the other end. The clamp's grip on the object is tightened by striking the wedge on a hard surface.

Hand vise. This small vise is hand-held. (See Fig. 16.) It is excellent for holding small pieces that need filing, for twisting heavy wire and similar jobs. Its serrated jaws should be covered with copper or aluminum in the same manner as the jaws of the bench vise.

FOR CUTTING AND DRILLING

Metal shears (also called "metal snips"). (See Fig. 17.) There are several types, but those labeled universal (aviation or compound action) and tinner's are best for cutting 18 ga. and thinner craft metals. A plate shear is a smaller version of the tinner's snips and is very useful for cutting small squares of sheet solder. Note that no metal shear or snip should be used for cutting wire, as it ruins the cutting edges.

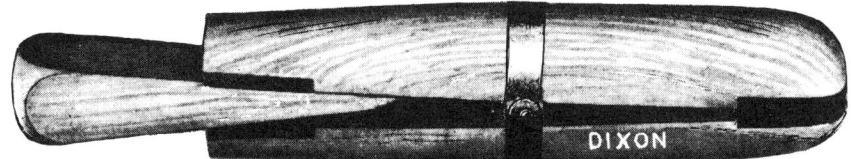

FIGURE 15

FIGURE 16

UNIVERSAL   TINNER'S   PLATE SHEAR

FIGURE 17

Jeweler's saw. This is probably the most used and most useful tool for jewelry making. (See Fig. 18.) An adjustable 3-in. or 4-in. frame is your best selection.

Jeweler's saw blades. These come in various sizes ranging from No. 8/0 (the thinnest, with the smallest teeth) to No. 14 (the thickest, with the largest teeth). (See Fig. 19.) Sizes 3/0, 2/0 and 0 are needed to cut the metals used in the projects in this book.

Beeswax. A small amount is useful for lubricating saw blades during the sawing practice.

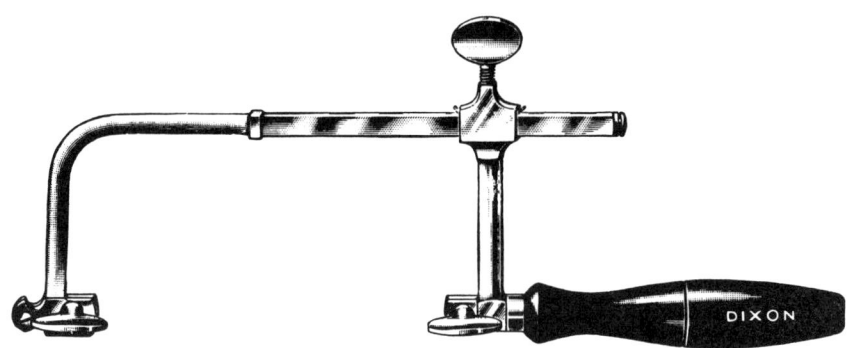

FIGURE 18

Size No.	Thickness	Width	Blades	Size No.	Thickness	Width	Blades
8/0	.006	.013	Saws Finer Than 4/0 Not Illustrated	2	.014	.027	
7/0	.007	.014		3	.014	.029	
6/0	.007	.014		4	.015	.031	
5/0	.008	.015		5	.016	.034	
4/0	.008	.017		6	.019	.041	
3/0	.010	.019		8	.020	.048	
2/0	.010	.020		10	.020	.058	
0	.011	.023		12	.023	.064	
1	.012	.025		14	.024	.068	
1½	.012	.025					

FIGURE 19

Hand drill. The type obtainable in any hardware store is quite acceptable and will give good service. A ¼-in. or ⅜-in. electric drill—or drill press, if you have one—will do most of the jobs of the hand drill, except—as you will see—that of twisting wire.

Twist drills (also called "bits"). These are available in number sizes (No. 80 the smallest to No. 1 the largest); in fractional sizes (1/64 in. to 1½ in. by increments of 1/64 inch); and in letter sizes (A to Z). The number sizes are the usual choice for jewelry handicrafting, and the sizes to get as a start are numbers 67, 60, 53, 45, 37, 30, 21, and 12. Either carbon steel or high-speed twist drills can be bought. The cutting edges of the high-speed drill last longer

GETTING STARTED

than the carbon steel, but high-speed bits are more brittle and, unless carefully handled, break easily. The choice is yours.

Cutting pliers (also called "nippers"). These are primarily used for cutting wire. (See Fig. 20.) Either the side or end cutting pliers illustrated (4½ in. to 5½ in. long, depending on the size of your hand) is all you need.

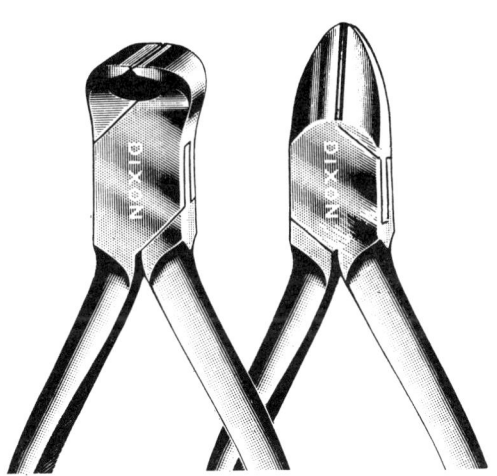

FIGURE 20

FOR MEASURING AND MARKING METAL

Rule (or ruler). A 6-in. or 12-in. steel rule with graduations down to 1/32 in. on one edge and graduations in millimeters and centimeters on the other edge is preferred. A good wooden ruler with these same graduations will also serve.

Steel scriber. This is used to scribe lines on metal. An ice pick, an awl, a sharply pointed 20-penny finishing nail, or any steel rod about 4 in. long and ⅛ in. in diameter will do. So will a heavy sewing needle centered, inserted and cemented (blunt end in) into a ¼-in. or ⅜-in. piece of wood dowel. When your scriber's point becomes dull through use, resharpen it on a sharpening stone and polish the point with the different grades of abrasive cloth listed below.

Center punch. This is basically the same shape and length as the scriber, but is about ¼ in. diameter and is used to indent spots on metal where a hole is to be drilled. The small identation provides a starting place for the twist drill without which the bit would wander across the metal's surface producing hard-to-remove blemishes along the way.

Hammer. Any lightweight utility hammer (carpenter's, tinsmith's, etc.) will do the trick. Reserve this hammer for rough use such as striking the center punch. Never use it to strike the craft metals directly, because any dents, scratches or other imperfections on its striking face will be faithfully reproduced in the metal. To eliminate these blemishes will generally require many hours of time and at least a half ton of elbow grease.

Divider. A double-pointed compass employed for such tasks as scribing arcs and circles on metal and for transferring measurements.

Compass. You will need an ordinary school-type compass for drawing jewelry designs on paper.

FOR FORMING, BENDING AND TEXTURING METAL

Ball peen hammer. A good choice is one weighing either 2 or 4 ounces. (See *A,* Fig. 21.)

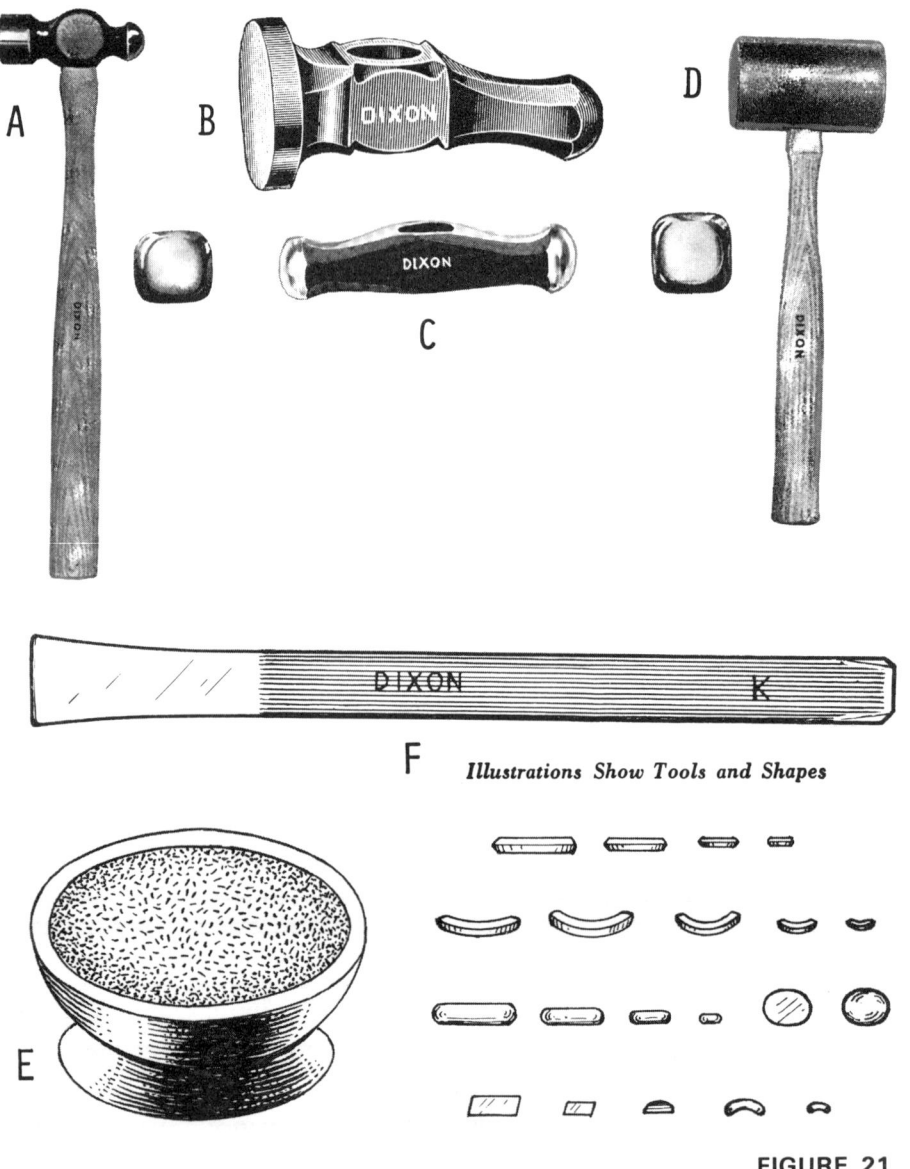

FIGURE 21

GETTING STARTED

Chasing hammer. One with a 1⅛-in. face. (See *B*, Fig. 21.)

Embossing hammer. Supplier's catalogs show embossing hammers with striking faces that differ in size and shape. The one illustrated here will do for the projects in this book. (See *C*, Fig. 21.)

Forming hammers are exclusively used to strike craft metals directly. The striking faces of these hammers—as well as the striking or supporting surfaces of every tool or item of equipment used in forming or texturing craft metals, including forming pliers—must be kept perfectly smooth, highly polished and free from rust. Directions are given in Chapter 3 for removing dents, pits, and scratches from metals. The same procedures are followed in keeping the above implements free from imperfections.

Rawhide mallet. This tool is used to hammer metal flat or to form it into various shapes. (See *D*, Fig. 21.) If used with rather light, flat-faced blows, it does its work without marring the metal. A fairly good substitute can be improvised by tying a 2 in. x 2 in. x ¼ in. or ⅛ in. piece of flexible leather, smooth side out, over the flat face of the chasing hammer.

Chaser's pitch. This material is used to hold metal in certain operations which are described in the next chapter. It is sold by jewelry supply houses either loose or in a container. (See *E*, Fig. 21.) A container of some sort is necessary to hold the pitch. The best is a cast-iron pitch bowl that is supported on a thick rubber or leather ring. A round or rectangular tin pie pan may also be used to hold the pitch.

Chasing tools. These can be purchased in sets or as individual pieces and are used for such decorative purposes as incising lines and forming depressions in metal. (See *F*, Fig. 21.) They can also be made in the home workshop, but the making requires time plus motor-driven grinding wheels. A small straight and a curved liner are all you will need to complete the projects in this book in which chasing is used.

Dapping punches. These tools are used with a hammer to dome metals and to produce shallow or deep depressions on the front or back surfaces of metal shapes. These may be utilized in conjunction with a steel dapping die or design block (see Fig. 22) as well as with a lead block, which is how we will employ them. They are sold in sets or as individual items and Numbers 28 (1 in.), 22 (⅞ in.), 19 (¾ in.), and 16 (⅝ in.) are good to have for a start. Dapping

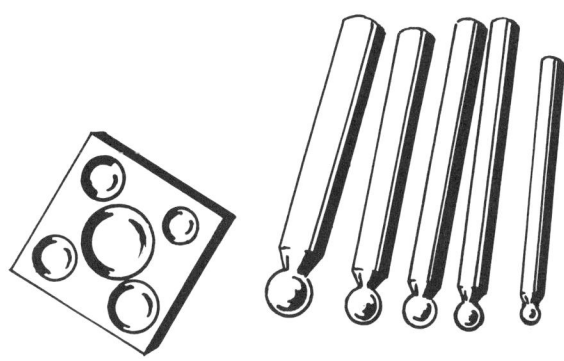

FIGURE 22

punches can be made by rounding and smoothing the ends of 4-in. lengths of steel rods or hardwood dowels of the appropriate diameters, making them as spherical as possible and free from any dents or other blemishes.

Bench anvil. A block of 4 in. x 4 in. x ½ in. to 1 in. steel with one smoothly polished top surface on which craft metals can be hammered for various purposes. An old-fashioned flat-iron or the base plate of a worn-out electric iron is an acceptable substitute. Either can be supported base up in the bench vise.

Lead block. This item of equipment, roughly 4 in. square by 1 in. thick (or, if round, 4 in. in diameter by 1 in. thick), is employed for a number of dapping and other forming operations. Many plumbing supply and hardware outlets sell lead in bar form, and several bars can be melted together on the kitchen stove in a small iron frying pan to a round shape of the desired thickness. Line the pan with 2 or 3 sheets of heavy household aluminum foil to keep the lead from contacting the frying pan's cooking surface and apply a thin coat of light machine oil to the foil to keep the lead from sticking. Whether you buy your block from a jewelry supply house or make your own, it is well to know how to remelt the lead since the block will become full of hollows, dents and other distortions after heavy use.

Brass bristle brush. This small, soft brush is similar to the kind used to clean suède shoes and other articles made of suède. While not a forming tool in itself, it is essential that it be used in connection with the lead block. Metal hammered on the block can pick up tiny particles of lead which, if not removed, will burn holes in the metal later if it is subjected to the annealing or soldering process. The brass brush removes these particles when the metal is scrubbed vigorously with it.

Forming pliers. Essential forming pliers—each about 5 in. to 5½ in. long—are the round nose, flat nose and chain nose (also referred to as needle or snipe nose). (See Fig. 23.) A

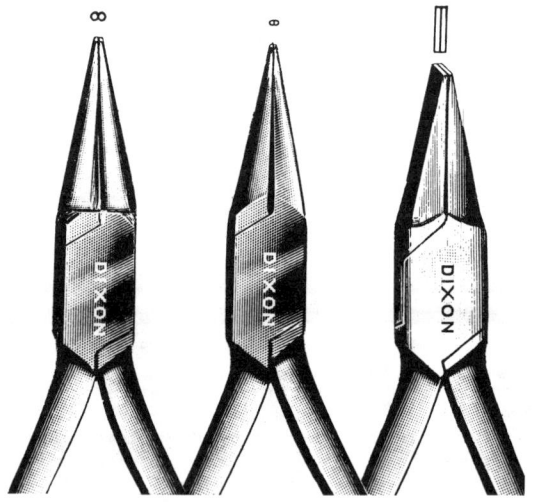

FIGURE 23

GETTING STARTED

good choice for the flat-nose pliers is the parallel action type in which the jaws open and close equidistantly along their entire length. This action results in fewer marks on the metal being held by the pliers. Jewelry-making pliers are commonly made with smooth jaws in contrast to pliers intended for electrical and electronic work which normally have serrated jaws like those on the bench vise. The little teeth on these pliers can be removed with a file and abrasive cloth in the manner later to be described for removing blemishes from craft metals. The operation must be done with care, however, so as not to leave a gap between the jaws of the pliers when they are closed.

Bracelet mandrel, round. This is used for rounding solid metal bracelets and other objects. The one shown in Fig. 24 (*A*) is 12 in. long and tapers from 1¾ in. at the top to 3½ in. at the bottom. An oval bracelet mandrel is also available with the same over-all dimensions. A round

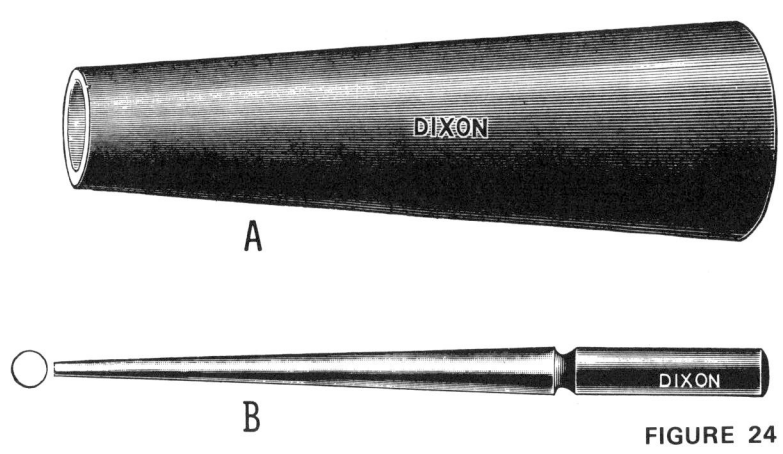

FIGURE 24

metal bracelet (in contrast to the flexible link type) can usually be pressed into shape by the judicious use of one's hands. Reasonable substitutes can be made for the round mandrel at little cost. You can use 6-in. lengths of hardwood dowels, wood or metal closet clothes poles, smoothly polished metal rods or stiff thick-walled sections of pipe—all in different diameters, ranging from 1¾ in. to 3½ in. Plumbing supply outlets will have short pieces of copper, brass and iron pipe. Metal food cans (*e.g.,* tomato paste, soup, etc.) with labels removed, cleaned inside and out, and solidly filled with hardened ready-mix cement (obtainable in most lumber yards) will also work, providing you avoid hammering the bracelet on the can's seam. With a little ingenuity, you probably can come up with many other improvisations.

Ring mandrel. This mandrel (see *B,* Fig. 24) has many uses, including the shaping, sizing and, if necessary, the stretching of finger rings; making bezels for the larger gemstones, large chain links and other similar items. A ring mandrel that has numbered graduations on it corresponding to ring sizes is the better choice. Since a ring, to be comfortable, must fit the wearer's finger quite exactly, attempting to find substitutes for the ring mandrel is impractical.

Bezel mandrel, round. A smaller version of the ring mandrel, it is employed in much the same way as the ring mandrel, but for standard-size bezels, chain links, rounding metal circles to be soldered on jewelry for decorative purposes, and the like. Again, inasmuch as bezels must closely fit the gemstones they are intended for, more time and effort can be spent in hunting for or devising a practical replacement for the mandrel than it is worth.

Ring sizer. This is used to measure fingers for rings by the trial and error method; *i.e.,* successive sizer rings are slipped on the finger which will wear the ring until the one that fits most comfortably is found. (See Fig. 25.) The number on each sizer ring corresponds to a number on the graduated ring mandrel, indicating where the ring you are creating should come to a stop in order to fit the wearer's finger. Do not invest in a ring sizer, however, until you try the alternatives given in the chapter on rings.

FIGURE 25

FOR MELTING, SOLDERING, ANNEALING, PICKLING AND COLORING METAL

The soldering process has already been partially explained. Since this will be gone into further in the next chapter along with the *why's* and *how's* of melting, annealing, pickling and coloring metals, space will not be taken here to explain the new terms.

Before listing the equipment that can serve as suitable heat sources for the above jewelry-making processes, a few points should be made. All melting, hard and soft soldering, and annealing of craft metals is almost always done with equipment that produces a flame. A small soldering iron (not the large, heavy tinsmith's kind) has some uses for the application of soft solder. The processes requiring the highest temperatures are metal melting and Hard-grade hard soldering, and to provide the high heat needed the flame should burn at a temperature of

GETTING STARTED

at least 2100 degrees, and preferably higher. Even though copper—which has the highest melting point of all the craft metals you will use—has a melting point of 1981 degrees, a flame of a higher-burning temperature still is needed since some of its heat is dissipated into the air surrounding the flame, and more is absorbed by the materials supporting and/or holding the metal being heated.

HEATING SOURCES FOR JEWELRY MAKING

Equipment is available that produces flames up to 6000 degrees, but this equipment involves large gas storage tanks or noisy air compressors, plus accessories—all of which can add up to a tidy outlay of money. This equipment is fine for the professional craftsman, and you will find it listed in some jewelry tool catalogs as well as being shown in places that sell welding apparatus. For you as a beginning craftsman, however, at least until you know how far you plan to go in the craft, the recommendations of heating equipment which follow will serve admirably.

Presto-O-Lite Soldering Unit. The commercial name is given here because, while there are other units similar to it, this make is probably the best known and most used by craftsmen. Two sizes of tanks filled with compressed acetylene gas are available. The gas, burned with oxygen in the air, produces a flame with a temperature of about 4000 degrees. There is a choice of stems for the torch handle. The fine stem is good for most soldering operations; the light, or medium, stem is better for melting metals, for large soldering jobs, for the annealing of fairly large pieces of metal, and for the hardening and tempering of steel tools you can make for yourself. While the initial money outlay for this unit is not inconsiderable (but still lower than the more sophisticated outfits), the operating cost is minimal. When necessary, you can exchange the empty tank for a full one, paying only a small amount for the gas.

Propane gas torch units. Three different types of torch are available, each costing much less than the acetylene unit. Each unit consists of a nonrefillable tank of gas (you discard it when exhausted and buy a fresh one), and a torch stem that produces a 2300-degree flame. The Bantam Unit provides a needlepoint flame good for small hard-soldering operations. The flame of the Master Unit is adjustable from needlepoint to larger, making it the more versatile torch. Since both units, when employed, are usually hand-held, the disadvantage of the Master Unit is that it is heavier to hold and clumsier to use. However, you can purchase a Master Unit with a flexible hose between the tank and torch handle that eliminates the need for hand-holding the tank. Being much smaller, propane gas tanks will obviously not give nearly as many hours of use as either of the acetylene gas tanks.

The equipment above will satisfactorily and, if used intelligently, safely perform all the melting, soldering and other heating operations you will be required to do. There are, however, some heating operations—such as the heating of liquids—which are better done by other means. The kitchen stove, if handy, will serve nicely. If its use is inconvenient, then the following items are suggested:

Bunsen burner. Bunsen burners are made for use with either natural or manufactured gas.

This item is appropriate for some soft-soldering operations, but is useful mainly for heating liquids. The liquid containers (preferably glass that can withstand heat) must be supported on some sort of heating frame—either the familiar tripod and iron mesh or the kind improvised from a two-quart can as shown in Fig. 26. In the latter, the large opening is cut with the metal shear and the holes on top are drilled or punched in with an ice pick or awl.

Electric hot plate. This is a small, portable electric stove which is useful only for heating liquids.

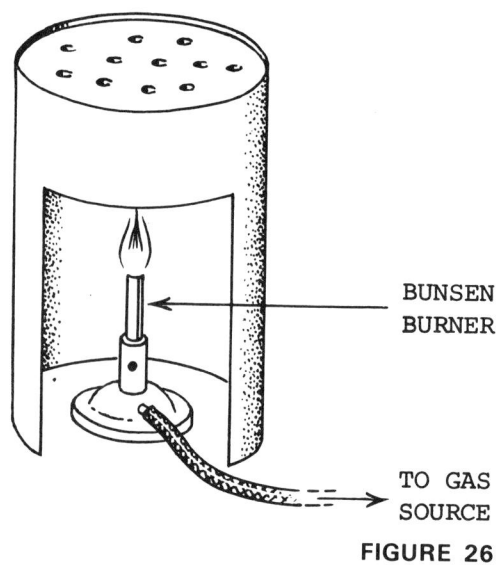

BUNSEN BURNER

TO GAS SOURCE

FIGURE 26

ACCESSORY EQUIPMENT

The following implements and supplies are virtually indispensable where heat is involved as part of a process or technique:

Flint striker. This is much safer to use than matches or a cigarette lighter to ignite the soldering torch and/or Bunsen burner.

Charcoal block. The most practical size is 4¾ in. x 3 in. This is specially prepared charcoal on which metal being annealed or hard soldered is placed. The block aids the heating process by reflecting the heat striking its surface back to the metal. In use, the block should always rest on the asbestos pad described in the last chapter. After some use, the block has a tendency to split across its width. This may be prevented by winding two or three strands of binding wire around a new block's perimeter (see Fig. 27) and making the wire taut by twisting the ends together with pliers.

Binding wire (soft, black, iron). Various gauges are sold on 4-oz. spools. Its principal use is in the binding together of work to be soldered. Its oxidized surface prevents solder from adhering to the wire. You are well supplied if you have one spool each of 18- and 26-gauge wire.

GETTING STARTED

FIGURE 27

Sparex No. 2. This is a granular compound which is mixed with water (instructions on each can) to prepare what is known as "pickle" or "pickle bath." The pickle does the job of removing hardened flux and oxides from metals, and Sparex is much safer to handle than the long familiar and still used sulfuric and nitric acid solutions.

Bottles or jars. Any quart size or larger glass or plastic container with a tight-fitting cover in which to store the pickle. The pickle used for copper and brass should be kept separate from that used with silver because some copper is dissolved in the solution as the metals are being cleansed of flux and oxides. If silver is put in the copper pickle, some copper may be deposited on the silver. Such a deposit is difficult to remove. When either bath has turned a fair shade of blue, it should be discarded and replaced with fresh pickle.

Pyrex pot or beaker. Small size, for heating pickle and other solutions.

Copper tongs. These are used to transport metal into and out of the pickle bath.

Yellow ochre or loam. When mixed with water to a thick creamy paste, this is often painted on a previously soldered joint to prevent the joint from being affected by the heat when a nearby joint is being soldered.

Camel's hair brushes. You will need at least three of the small, inexpensive water-color type; one for applying soft solder flux, another for hard solder flux, and the third for applying coloring solutions and yellow ochre to metal. The brushes should be washed carefully after each use.

Crosslock tweezers, w/blunt points. These are quite useful for holding metal parts together during some soldering operations. (See *A,* Fig. 28.)

Plain tweezers. Employed for handling small pieces of metal or solder. (See *B,* Fig. 28.)

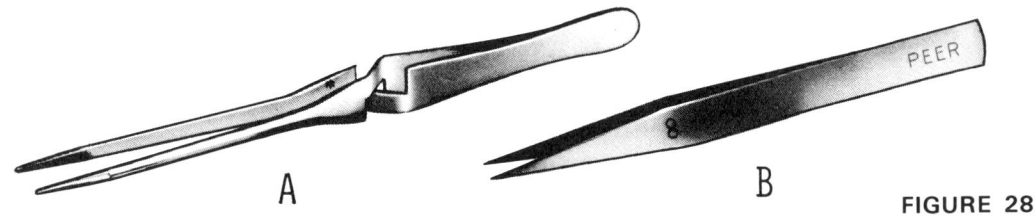

FIGURE 28

Hollow scraper. A handy tool for removing excess solder (particularly soft solder) from metal. (See Fig. 29.)

Liver of sulfur (potassium sulfide). This chemical, used for coloring metals, is available from jewelry supply houses and most local pharmacies. A 2-ounce supply is sufficient at first, but be sure to store it in a dark bottle in a dark place otherwise it deteriorates quite rapidly. A further warning: the stuff smells awful, like rotten eggs. Discard the solution after use, it does not last.

FIGURE 29

FOR FILING, BUFFING AND POLISHING METAL

Regular files. For jewelry making, the Swiss pattern files are considered superior to all other patterns both in their performance and in their lasting qualities. Files with tangs (the part that goes into a handle) are measured by the length of their cutting section, and those that measure 6 inches are recommended. Swiss files are available in a number of different "cuts," the "cut" being a measure of a file's coarseness or smoothness, with No. 0 the coarsest and No. 4 the smoothest. Tanged files come in many shapes, but a No. 2 cut and a No. 4 cut in the half round ring and round file are suggested as a start. If you already have some files of any cut, pattern or shape, by all means see if they meet your needs before investing in others.

Since you will be using files about as much as any other tool, a special word should be said about their care. No tanged file should be employed without a handle. Never pound or hammer the end of a file to seat the tang in the handle. Instead, slip the right-sized handle over the tang and gently force the file as far as possible into the hole. Then wind some cloth around the file's cutting section to protect your hand, grasp the file and, while holding it in a vertical position, tap the handle on a hard surface until the tang is firmly seated. To prolong the life of *all* files, never toss them into a drawer or other container or in a pile on the workbench. Devise a way to hang them up or set them in a row of holes drilled in wood. Do not oil files, but do keep them dry and in a dry place, as rust crumbles the teeth away.

Needle files. These files are used in places too small for the larger files to reach. Needle files are made in at least a dozen different shapes, but those recommended for a beginner are the knife, round, half round and square. The size of these files is determined by their over-all length, which includes the knurled handle. Those 5½ in. long with cuts No. 2 and No. 4 are suggested for each of the recommended shapes.

Abrasive cloths or papers. These are used to sand or abrade away pits, scratches and other blemishes on craft metals as well as on tools and equipment. The standard abrasives for metals

GETTING STARTED

are emery paper and cloth and aluminum oxide paper and cloth. Cloth-backed abrasives last much longer than the paper-backed. Both the paper- and cloth-backed abrasives come 9 in. wide. They are easier to handle if divided and cut the 9 in. way into six 1½-in. strips. Each strip can then be cut to the length needed. Be sure to label each strip with its grit size and keep each size separate from the others. Do not throw a strip away as the grit wears down. Instead, relabel it to the next finer grit size and keep doing that until it is almost completely worn out. Each type is made in different size grits, and for reasons best known to their manufacturers, each make, by and large, has a different code to designate the grit size. The grades shown below *on the same line* are more or less equivalent to each other. Having one sheet of each grade from the *same column* will give you the grit sizes you ought to have on hand.

CODE 1		CODE 2		CODE 3
Coarse	=	No. 2	=	No. 180
Medium	=	No. 1	=	No. 240
Medium Fine	=	No. 2/0	=	No. 320
Fine	=	No. 3/0	=	No. 400
Very Fine	=	No. 4/0	=	No. 500

Crocus cloth. This stands alone as the finest grade of all the abrasives and is used only for final polishing.

Scotch stone. This stone is used wet to remove dents and scratches that are hard to reach with a file or abrasive cloth or paper. Because it is soft, the stone soon wears down to the contour of the surface being worked on. Also, you can file the end of the stone to any desired contour. A stone 5 in. long by ¼ in. square is a convenient size to have around.

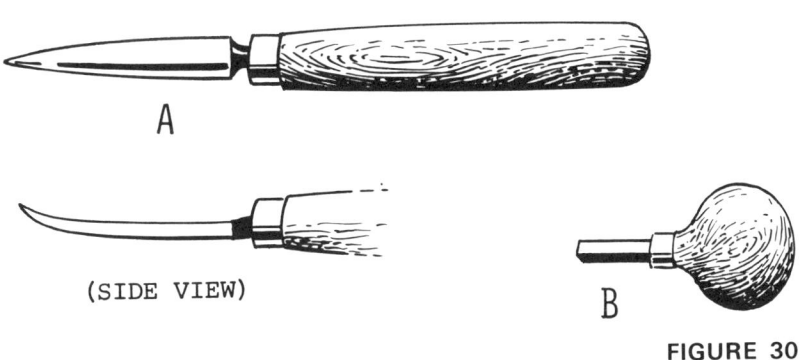

FIGURE 30

Burnisher. (See *A,* Fig. 30.) Extremely handy for smoothing the bezel around a gemstone, for smoothing and polishing metal in hard-to-reach places, and even, sometimes, to obtain a different surface effect. The curved style is recommended.

Stone pusher. (See *B,* Fig. 30.) Used for pushing the bezel over the stone before using the burnisher.

Tripoli compound. A buffing (smoothing) material used to remove the very fine scratches left on metal by even the finest abrasives and the marks left by the Scotch stone. A ¼-lb. cake is sold by some suppliers; others offer only a 1-lb. bar. A quarter pound of tripoli goes a long, long way.

Felt polishing stick (hand buff). (See Fig. 31.) Tripoli compound, rubbed on the felt, is applied to the metal. You can make your own buff with a piece of wood 10½ in. x ⅞ in. x ¼ in. thick on which a strip of felt 6 in. x ⅞ in. and from ⅛ in. to ¼ in. thick is glued. The glue must not be permitted to soak through to the top (rubbing) surface of the felt.

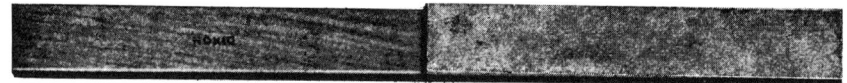

FIGURE 31

Red jeweler's rouge. This produces a bright, mirrorlike finish on all craft metals. A ¼-lb. stick or bar is sufficient for a hundred or more pieces of jewelry.

Chamois polishing stick (hand buff). This is used to apply jeweler's rouge to metal; its dimensions can be the same as the felt stick (above), and you can make your own by simply using a piece of chamois instead of felt. *Important:* Never apply rouge to a tripoli buff or tripoli to a rouge buff. The mixup can cause such a mess that the contaminated objects may have to be discarded.

Washout brush. Jewelry articles must often be thoroughly washed with soap or a detergent and rinsed before proceeding from one step to the next. Excellent brushes for this purpose are available, but a long-used hand or fingernail brush, toothbrush or similar brush with medium-hard bristles will work just as well.

MOTORIZED EQUIPMENT?

No listing of tools and equipment that are good to have, even at the start, would really be complete without some mention of the advantages in having motorized equipment plus the many accessories and attachments, especially those for smoothing and polishing operations. Using motor-driven buffing and polishing wheels not only reduces the time it takes to do these operations, but the end result is usually much better. One reason for not strongly promoting motors and motorized items is our effort to keep the beginner's initial investment down to an acceptable sum. The other—and unquestionably the stronger reason—is that unless one learns how to use the larger motors (not the small hand-held types), particularly in relation to jewelry making, they can be quite dangerous and often self-defeating in terms of their purpose. It is recommended that you consult books that deal with motorized polishing or else consult someone experienced in the process who can show you the dos and don'ts before you attempt it yourself. Motors are mentioned here because the author's own experi-

GETTING STARTED

ence in using the considerable amount of motorized equipment in his own shop has convinced him of the advantages inherent in using such equipment as soon as you can.

Most complete jewelry tool and supply catalogs show a variety of motors and hundreds of time- and worksaving attachments and accessories that can be used with such motors. The suggestion is that you study the catalog sections in which these attachments and accessories are illustrated and explained. The descriptions supplied with the articles generally will contain enough information for you to understand the *how, what* and *why* of each item. You will find small hand-held motors and flexible shaft machines that are safe for anyone to use. A flexible shaft machine can be contrived by combining a functioning electric sewing machine motor—or any 1/15th or 1/10th horsepower electric motor—with an item sold under the trade name of Flexade. And if you have, or can buy, the foot-operated rheostat that varies the speed of the motor, you are really in clover. The author has such a flexible shaft outfit driven by a motor from an old window fan.

When you are ready to use the kind of equipment driven by the higher-powered electric motors—$1/8$th to $1/2$ horsepower types—you may find that you have such a motor lying around in your basement. If not, investigate electric motor repair shops in your area. They sometimes have rebuilt motors that sell for much less than new ones. Also visit shops that repair household electric appliances (refrigerators, washing machines, clothes dryers, and such) as well as firms that install home furnaces and central air conditioning systems. They sometimes have used motors that still operate which they will sell for a few dollars. Even if a motor requires some reconditioning, this can usually be done by an electric motor repair shop for a nominal charge. These can be fitted with tapered spindles on which it becomes a simple matter to mount polishing buffs and brushes made specifically for motorized equipment.

3/MASTERING BASIC TECHNIQUES

This chapter will demonstrate and explain only the basic processes involved in making jewelry. Variations of these basic techniques will be covered as they are used in the projects. First, cut some 2- to 3-inch by 1- to 2-inch pieces from your 16- and 18-gauge copper and brass as you will need them in trying your hand at each process that follows. Do this cutting only after reading the section below on Cutting Craft Metal. You can probably use each of these pieces for practice in more than one process. Afterwards do not throw the pieces away. They will be useful later for making beads and other decorative objects.

Transferring Designs to Metal

Most articles of jewelry start out as a design drawn on paper with a pencil. For this initial step a good quality tracing paper is recommended. Once you, the craftsman, are satisfied with your design, it is best to go over all of its details with a fine pen and India ink because the pencil drawings will soon become smudged with handling. Then proceed to transfer the design to the metal you plan on using. There are a variety of transfer methods, but those described here are the simplest. In each method the metal should be: (*a*) scrubbed with the kind of household cleanser employed on kitchen sinks, or rubbed with a piece of fine sanding cloth or fine steel wool; (*b*) washed with a soap or detergent and water solution to which a little household ammonia has been added; (*c*) rinsed in clean water, and (*d*) dried with a clean cloth. The purpose of all this is to remove any oxides, grease and/or oil that may be on the metal. From this point on, it is wise to handle the metal only by the edges so as not to contaminate its surface with the natural oil on your fingers and hands.

Most designs are generally not complicated, and you can simply glue the paper containing the drawing to the metal with a water-soluble glue or rubber cement. This method works, however, only when a *one-of-a-kind* jewelry article is to be made. When more than one of a kind is desired or needed—*e.g.,* matching earrings—then the original drawing must be duplicated by tracing it on a second sheet of tracing paper. As a rule, all cutting and drilling *inside* the over-all form of the design is done first; the cutting of the *outline* of the form itself is done last. Once all operations are completed, the paper remaining on the metal can be removed thusly: (1) water-soluble glue can be dissolved in warm water; (2) paper fixed to metal with rubber cement can be peeled off, and any cement remaining may be rubbed off with a clean cloth, or (3) in either case the paper and glue or cement can be burned off with the torch.

Another design transfer technique employs white tempera (poster, show-card) paint which is brushed on the thoroughly cleansed metal. If the tempera does not brush out evenly, but collects in small globules, the metal has not been properly cleaned. You have a choice between two paths to take with the tempera method. In one, you place a piece of black or red carbon (typing) paper on a perfectly smooth and flat surface, carbon side up. Over this, place your paper with the design, design side up. Then you completely retrace the drawing with a *sharp* and *hard* lead pencil so that carbon is deposited on the reverse side of the paper. With the tempera dry, the paper is placed on the metal with the carbon side down, and you once again retrace every detail of your drawing with the same sharp, hard pencil. When you remove the paper the entire design should be clearly visible on the white paint. You now use your scriber to scratch (lightly) the design through the paint onto the metal. Lightly is emphasized because, if the scriber slips and makes a mistake, deep scratches are difficult to remove. The tempera is washed away with water, leaving the design inscribed on the metal.

The second tempera approach is slightly different from the first. In this, the carbon paper is placed, carbon side down, directly on the painted metal with the drawing on top of the carbon. The design is then retraced with the pencil, thus depositing carbon details on the tempera. The steps which follow are the same as in the first tempera approach.

The advantage of the first approach is that the metal's outline can easily be seen through the tracing paper so that the drawing can be placed exactly where it should go. The advantage of the second version is that one step is eliminated. In either procedure masking or cellulose tape can be used to hold the paper or papers on the metal.

Drilling Craft Metals

When metal is to be drilled, you should first scribe a tiny "x" on the precise spot where the twist drill is to enter the metal. Next, with the metal set on the bench anvil, indent the metal for the bit's point by placing your center punch on the spot where the lines forming the "x" cross. Then sharply strike the vertically held punch with the utility hammer. Do this for each hole to be drilled. When ready to drill, place the metal on a block

MASTERING BASIC TECHNIQUES

of wood that is larger than the metal. Figure 32 illustrates three ways to keep the metal from turning during the drilling process. In *A,* the metal is clamped by a C-clamp between the block of wood and a small, thin piece of wood to keep the clamp from marring the metal's surface. In *B,* small nails are driven into a block of wood around the edges of the metal. In *C* the metal and block are held by the shielded vise jaws.

In drilling, always hold the drill perpendicular to the metal, otherwise the bit's point will creep out of the indentation and scar the metal's surface. Also, excessive pressure can cause carbon steel twist drills to bend out of shape and high-speed drills to break. Lubricating the bit by turning its tip in the cake of beeswax not only makes the drilling process easier but prolongs the bit's life. Drilling large holes can be made easier by first drilling the hole with a small-sized bit and then following with the required size. The metal being drilled is backed with a block of wood to reduce the development of burrs on the reverse surface of the metal when the drill breaks through the metal. If burrs still occur, an easy way to remove them is to turn the metal over, secure it as before, and drill the burr off using a bit slightly larger than the one that made the hole. Do this slowly and gently so as not to enlarge the hole itself. Occasionally a bit will bind in the metal. Forcing it—the small sizes particularly—can result in a broken drill. It is better to back the bit out of the metal by turning it counterclockwise and then start again at reduced speed.

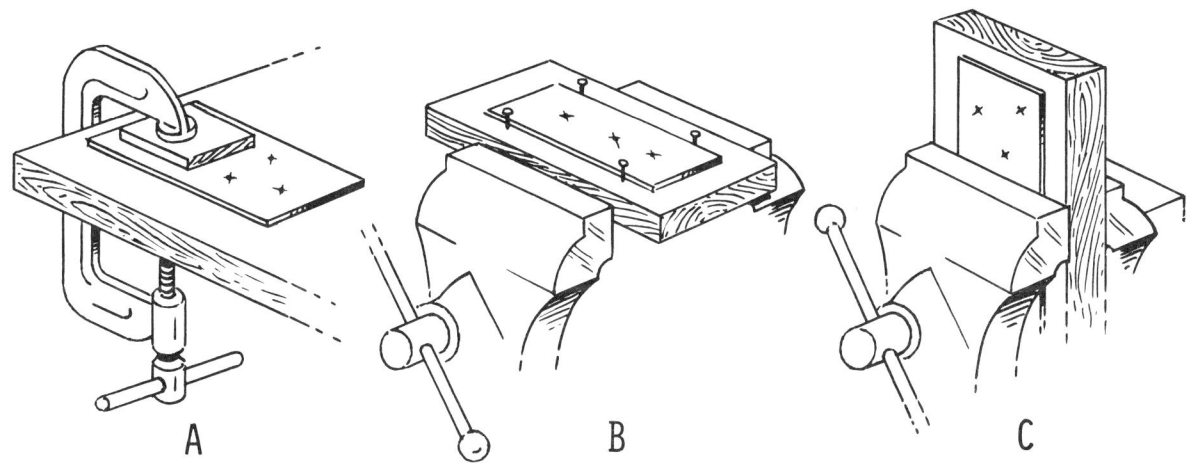

FIGURE 32

Cutting Craft Metals

USING METAL SHEARS

Metal shears, or snips, are primarily suitable for cutting large sheet stock into smaller sections. They are limited to thicknesses of metal no greater than 16 ga. The plate shears are mainly used for cutting hard sheet solder, bezel strips and 24-ga. and thinner sheet metal to size. All cutting with metal shears should be done with the rear of the jaws and never with the points. In cutting, open the shears' jaws as wide as possible and thrust the metal as far back between the jaws as you can. If you are cutting to a scribed line, line up the cutting edge of the upper jaw with the line and, while holding the shears perpendicular to the metal, make your cut to about the midpoint of the jaws and stop. Open the jaws wide again, thrust the metal back and continue this procedure until the full cut is made. The points of the jaws are not used because they tend to leave a ragged edge as they break through the metal.

In cutting 18-ga. and 16-ga. metal, you can obtain greater leverage by resting the lower handle of the shears on the workbench or by fastening the straight portion of this handle in your bench vise (remove the jaw shields first). In cutting long strips, it is usually necessary to bend the metal away from your hand holding the shears. Once the piece is cut, it can be straightened by placing it on your bench anvil and striking it with the full, flat face of your rawhide mallet.

USING THE JEWELER'S SAW

The first step to be taken with the jeweler's saw is to adjust its frame to a suitable length. This adjustment entails a number of steps. First—with a No. 0 saw blade handy—place the saw frame in a horizontal position against the edge of the workbench. Press your stomach against the saw's handle, using only sufficient pressure to hold the frame steady and in place. It is important to point out that the saw blade is always placed in the frame with its teeth pointing *outward,* away from the frame, and *downward* toward the handle. With this rule in mind loosen the upper clamp (the clamp on the part of the frame resting against the workbench) with your right hand and insert the appropriate end of the blade in the clamp with your left hand. About 1 inch of the blade's end should extend into the upper clamp. Holding the blade with your left hand as nearly parallel with the back of the saw frame as you can, tighten the clamp with your right hand.

Now hold the saw up in a vertical position to make certain the blade is in straight—that is, parallel to the back of the saw frame. If it slants toward or away from that part of the saw, you will have to repeat the above procedure until the blade is correctly aligned. Improper insertion of blade into the frame is one great cause of blade breakage. Next loosen the lower clamp and place the free end of the blade in the clamp. About ½-inch of this end should extend into the clamp. If the extension is much more or less than ½-in, loosen the thumbscrew on the back of the frame and adjust the frame as needed until the prescribed length of the blade rests within the lower clamp. Tighten the frame's thumbscrew securely. Its length should now be right for almost any saw blade you may insert into the frame, since most jeweler's blades are about 5-inches long.

Return the saw to the same position in which it was previously held between the workbench and your body. Make certain the blade's free end rests in the lower clamp. Grasp the saw's handle with your left hand and, with this hand and your body, exert pressure against the handle until this free end extends from ⅝-inch to ⅞-inch inside the clamp. When it does, tighten the clamp with your right hand and release your pressure on the frame. The blade, to

MASTERING BASIC TECHNIQUES

do its work, must be under fairly high tension. You can test for the correct tension by plucking the blade with a finger. If a high musical ping is produced, the blade is properly fixed; if you hear a low, mushy tone, the blade must be reset in the clamps. Not having a blade taut or having it too taut can be a major cause of blade breakage.

Metal to be cut with the jeweler's saw is supported on the bench pin with the line to be sawed always held over the V slot. We are starting with an outside cut—that is, cutting a piece of metal to the over-all shape of a jewelry design. To make the sawing easier, run the saw blade lightly over the cake of beeswax before you start. Occasionally rub the cake on the blade even while the latter is deep in a cut. Too much wax, however, tends to clog the teeth, and the excess should be removed with a bristle brush.

General note: The saw cuts only on the down stroke, and the blade tends to skid around when you start cutting from the edge of a piece of metal. There are two ways to avoid this: (1) make a little nick at the line by running the blade's teeth *upward* against the metal, or (2) nick the metal at the line with the thin edge of your knife-shaped needle file.

Take a comfortable seated position in front of the bench pin. The pin should be about 6 inches below your shoulder. Hold the metal on the pin with one hand and the saw with the other. Successful sawing (and less blade breakage) is highly dependent upon your strict adherence to these rules:

1. The saw must always be kept perpendicular to the top surface of the metal (see Fig. 33). When the saw is held at an angle, it becomes pinched—especially in sawing tight curves—and then, being thin, brittle and under tension, it snaps easily.

2. Saw on the outside of the line (in the part of the metal that will be waste), and not *on* the line. This leaves a little excess metal to be filed and sanded away in cleaning up the marks

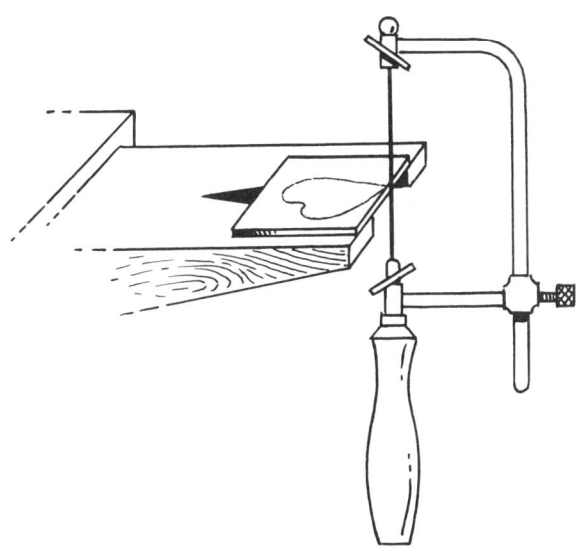

FIGURE 33

left by the saw. Cutting on or inside the line can result in changing the size and outline of the form you initially planned.

3. The saw is operated by holding the arm with the saw close to your side and steadily moving the arm up and down from the elbow, not the shoulder. It cannot be said that the saw should *never* be turned from its straight ahead, vertical position, but, in cutting a curved line or a full circle, it is *safer* if the metal is directed *into* the saw by the hand holding it rather than vice versa. There is then less chance of overtwisting the blade and thus breaking it.

4. Operate the saw gently; avoid excessive forward or downward force. The action of the blade's teeth serve to keep the saw moving forward, and the weight of the saw frame and your hand is sufficient to pull the blade down through the metal. Also, use the full length of the blade as much as possible.

5. One way to cut an angle (see Fig. 34) is to saw to the point of the angle and then "dance" the saw up and down without letting it move forward—much as if you were marking time in place with your feet. Meanwhile, turn the metal *slowly* until the angle's uncut side is in line with the blade, then let the saw move forward again.

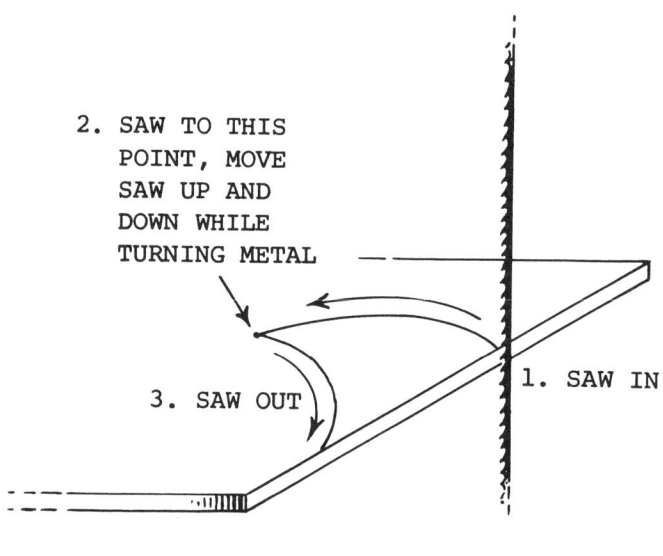

FIGURE 34

6. Another way to cut angles—particularly when you want the points where the sides meet to be really sharp—is to back the saw out of the first cut and come back at the angle from another direction (see Fig. 35). Backing a saw blade out of a cut is always a delicate maneuver, especially if long, intricate lines must be retraced. Rather than having the blade become pinched and perhaps broken, the safer approach is to loosen the saw's lower clamp and gently lift the blade out of the cut. Then reset the blade in the lower clamp and go at the angle from a different direction.

MASTERING BASIC TECHNIQUES 57

7. Blades become dull with use. Intricate cutting requires a sharp blade.

8. As a jewelry craftsman you will be doing a great amount of sawing. So relax. Take your time. Easy does it.

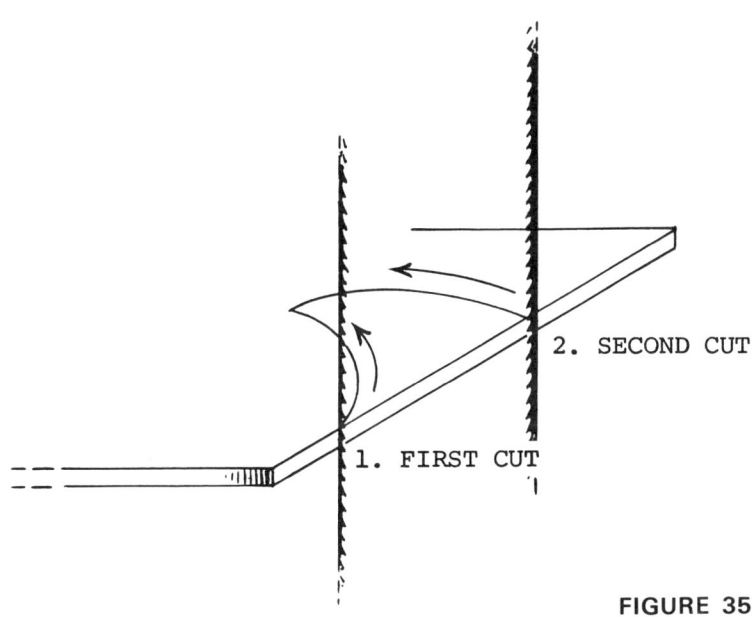

FIGURE 35

PIERCING

So far we have been discussing sawing on the outside, or waste side, of a jewelry form. But jewelry designs often call for cutting shapes out from *within* the form in an operation called *piercing*. The rules which apply to cutting on the outside of a form apply as well to inside cutting, but the question is: how do you get the saw blade in there without cutting your way in from the outer edge? The answer: by drilling a small hole in the portion of the metal to be cut out (the waste portion) through which the saw blade can be threaded. Figure 36 is an example of a form in which piercing is to be an aspect of the jewelry's over-all design. The x's shown not only mark the spaces that are to be cut out, but also indicate where the metal should be center-punched and drilled. A No. 0 or No. 2/0 saw blade is generally used for sawing 20-ga. and thicker metals, and a No. 60 twist drill provides a large enough hole to accept this size of blade. For piercing thinner metals or for cutting out tiny areas, it is better to use a 3/0 blade.

After the holes are drilled and the burrs, if any, are removed, the next step is to clamp the blade you have selected in the saw's upper clamp in the manner described earlier. Then thread the blade's free end into one of the drilled holes, design side of the metal facing the upper clamp, and move the metal as close to this clamp as possible. Follow by fixing the blade's free end in the lower clamp and under tension, just as for outside cutting. Then, grasping the metal

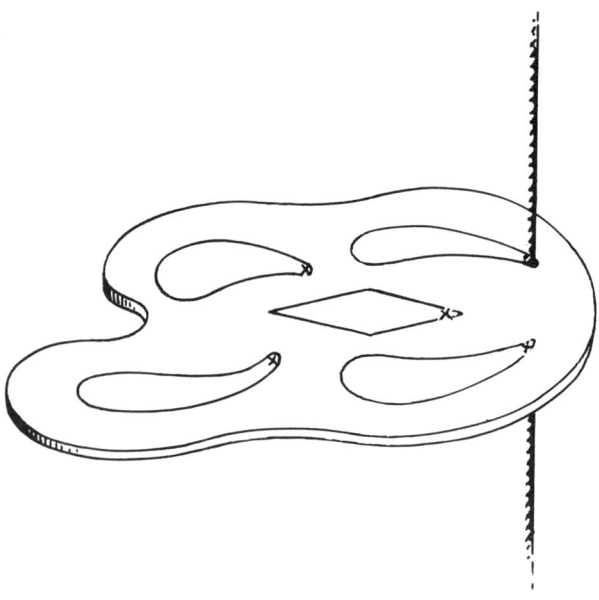

FIGURE 36

with one hand, carefully slide it down to the lower clamp and—with one hand holding the metal, the other the saw—place the metal over the V-slot of the bench pin. The sawing process from this point on follows all the rules described above, including those for cutting sharp curves and angles. When one section has been cut out, free the blade from the lower clamp and thread it through another hole and proceed as before.

Marks left by the saw's teeth are generally removed from the metal by files. Some designs, however, will require the piercing of sections too small to permit the entry of even the smallest file. There are two ways to handle this problem. One is to use the saw blade itself as a file. The blade's teeth are "set" so that each tooth is turned in a direction opposite to that of its immediate neighbors. This can easily be seen under a magnifying glass. The purpose of this is to have the blade cut a path (called "kerf") that is slightly wider than the thickness of the blade itself, which keeps the blade from binding in the cut. Rubbing the *sides* of the teeth up and down against the marks left by the blade will remove most of the saw marks. A second approach is known as "thrumming." In this, a strong piece of string is coated with tripoli compound. The string is threaded into the pierced opening and pulled back and forth—adding more tripoli compound as needed—until the walls of the opening are smooth.

Filing Metals

Files are used to smooth the flat and edge surfaces of metals and to refine a jewelry shape, particularly after sawing. If the sawing was done properly only a little filing will be necessary to true up the shape. Depending upon the amount of filing that has to be

MASTERING BASIC TECHNIQUES

done, start the operation with the coarser files and finish with your smoother files. This generally saves time and energy in the long run. It is important to keep in mind that the cutting edges of the teeth of all files point away from the file's handle. Thus, files cut only on the forward stroke. For efficient filing, therefore, and for the longer life of these tools, you should apply pressure only on the forward stroke. Develop the habit of lifting the file at the end of the forward stroke and carrying it back to the start of the stroke. Even dragging the tool lightly over the metal will eventually result in dulling its teeth.

All the file's teeth—from the tip to where the handle part begins—should, as a rule, be brought into contact with the surface being smoothed. Much filing can be done while using the bench pin to support the work. Depending on the size of the metal to be filed, work also can be held in the hand vise or in the ring clamp. Where long, straight edges have to be filed, it is best to clamp the work in the protected jaws of the bench vise. Both hands should be used in this type of smoothing operation—one on the end of the file and one on the handle. Whether smoothing a flat surface of a metal or an edge, the file should be moved forward diagonally (at a slant) across the metal (see Fig. 37) rather than straight across it. The latter action usually

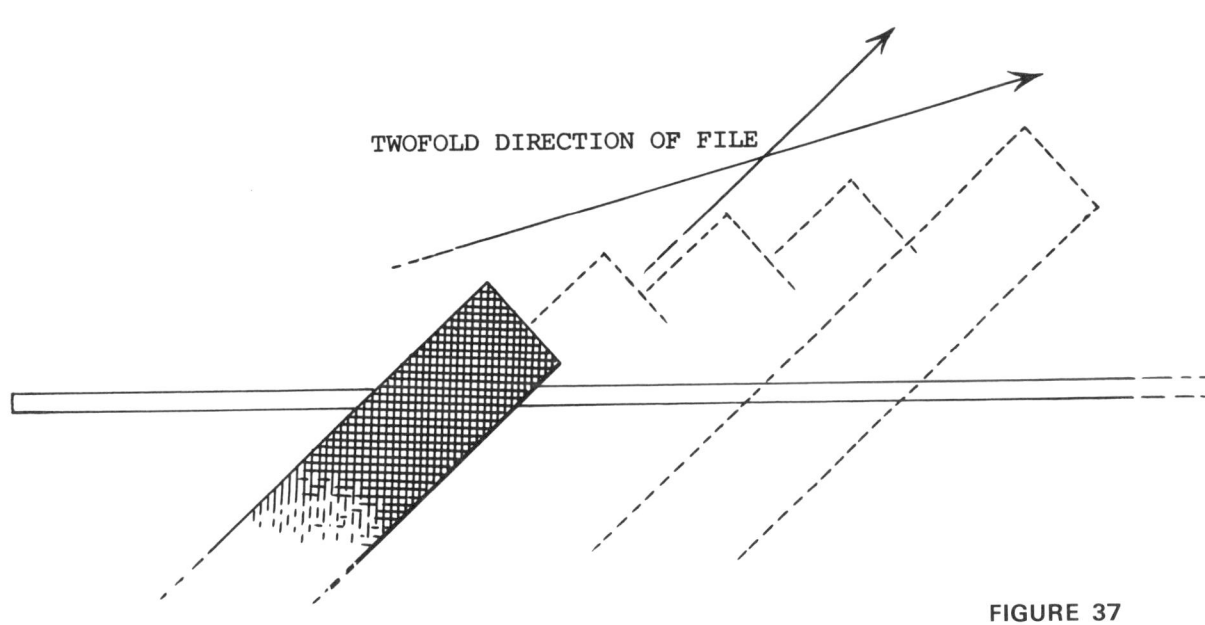

FIGURE 37

not only causes the file to chatter, but also has a tendency to leave high and low spots on the metal. The slanted stroke should be as long as possible in order to obtain the best results. Where two or more metal pieces are to be filed to the same shape and dimensions, the pieces can be secured in the bench or hand vise. By judiciously moving them around in either vise, all the pieces can be filed to identical shape and size.

Outside curves are usually filed with the *flat* side of the ring file, a flat needle file, or any other flat file you may have. Inside curves are filed with the round side of the ring file or half round or round needle file. It is difficult to prescribe which size of file to use in every case, since the size of the surface to be smoothed will tend to govern the size of the file that can be comfortably and effectively employed. The rule of thumb is to use the largest file that will do the work properly and without damage to the metal or the design. Filing generally leaves a burr on the corners where two surfaces of the metal being filed meet. Burrs are removed by holding the file at an angle to them and sliding it along in the same diagonal way as for regular filing. Removing the burrs will tend to round off these corners. How much to round off the meeting surfaces will depend upon the design of the jewelry. Some designs will look better with sharp, crisp edges; others with edges that are rounded off.

Small particles of metal will begin to clog your files after a certain amount of use with soft metals like copper, brass and silver. One way to reduce or even prevent this clogging is to rub a piece of blackboard chalk against the teeth of the file. This leaves little room for the particles of metal to get caught between the teeth, but does not keep the teeth from cutting. This procedure is fine with copper and brass, but it cannot be used with silver if you plan to sell your silver dust to a refiner. The chalk dust cannot be separated from the silver dust and this materially reduces its value. A file can be cleaned, instead, with a steel bristle brush—called a file card—which is run across the teeth to dislodge the particles clogging the teeth. Another way is to take a piece of scrap copper and run it across the teeth (in line with them). The copper soon takes on the shape of the rows of teeth and removes most of the particles. In each declogging procedure, the more stubborn bits can be picked out with a sharp pin, nail or awl.

HOLLOW SCRAPER

This is as good a place as any to talk about the hollow scraper. This tool is primarily employed to remove excess solder—soft solder, especially—from a craft metal after a soldering operation. A file should never be used on lead or lead solder because microscopic bits of lead can remain unseen on the teeth of the file and if such bits of lead should be transferred to a metal that is to be annealed or hard soldered, they will produce the disastrous pits and holes described in the last chapter. When using the scraper, keep one flat side of it as parallel to the surface being scraped as possible, otherwise the tool will chatter and produce ugly marks that are hard to eradicate. If the scraper is used properly and is kept sharp (hone it with a little oil on an oilstone), it will easily shave away excess solder and leave a surface that sanding cloth and the Scotch stone can further smooth.

Chasing Metals

Chasing—the process by which the *front* of an article is decorated or formed—can be a complicated but very artistic technique if performed to its fullest potential. This book gives a basic introduction to the technique so that you will be aware of its possi-

MASTERING BASIC TECHNIQUES

bilities as a decorative process. It is suggested that you practice this exercise with a piece of clean 18-ga. copper. Draw or transfer a leaf such as that shown in Figure 38, using one of the transfer methods described earlier in this chapter. You will need the chasing hammer, the curved and straight chasing liners, and the chaser's pitch—all of which were discussed in the previous chapter. Once you have done this exercise, you may wish to chase another design—a different leaf, a fish or the head of a dog for example. Also, in two later projects, we will use a different leaf motif to make silver earrings and a pin.

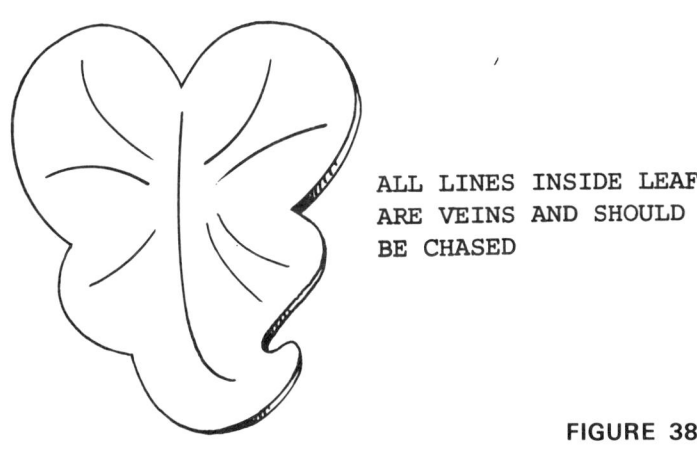

ALL LINES INSIDE LEAF ARE VEINS AND SHOULD BE CHASED

FIGURE 38

The first step in the chasing process is to transfer the design to metal and cut out the leaf with your jeweler's saw (no. 2/0 blade), then smooth and true the edges with your files. Next, fix the leaf onto the pitch. Do this by passing the soft flame of your torch over the surface of the pitch to soften it. Keep the torch moving so that the pitch, which is volatile, does not burn, as this will reduce its adhesiveness. When the pitch appears soft, press the metal, design side up, into it to a depth about equal to the thickness of the metal. With a moistened finger, press a little of the pitch over the edges of the copper to make the metal as secure as possible. Let the pitch cool and harden. The hardened pitch provides a backing that is sturdy enough to support the metal yet flexible enough to allow the latter to be indented.

The leaf's main vein is chased first, so have it facing you lengthwise. The lining tool is lightly grasped between the thumb and the first three fingers of one hand. The little finger may act as a support and guide for the hand by having it rest on the surface of the pitch. The length of the liner's chisel-like blade is held in line with the vein. Place the blade at the part of the vein farthest from you (you work toward yourself always) and tilt the tool's top away from you so that a part of its blade rests on the work. Grasp the chasing hammer in your other hand and strike the liner with steady, rhythmic and fairly light blows (see Fig. 39). If the tool is held and struck correctly it will move slightly forward with each blow. Do not force

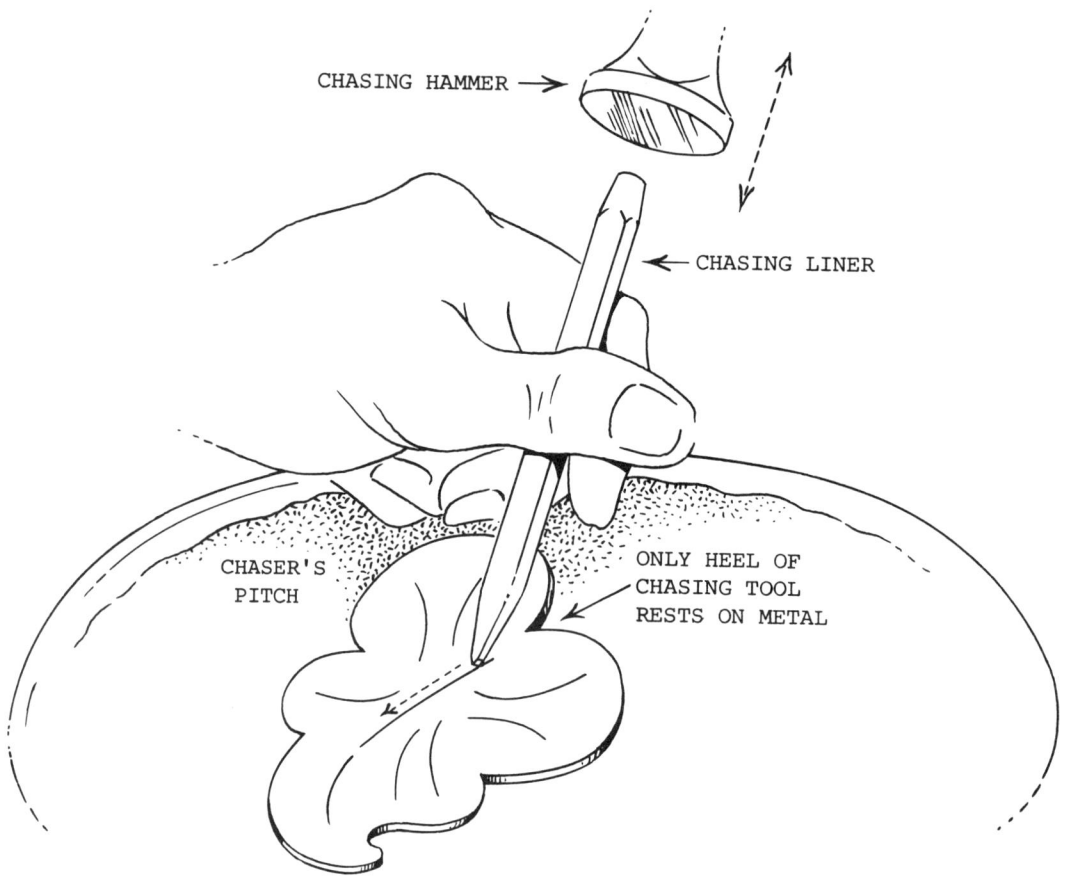

FIGURE 39

it forward; let the tools do the work. Keep the blows fairly rapid and light; remember you are only trying to indent the metal, not to cut it entirely through. Try to incise the entire line in one operation, *i.e.*, without lifting the liner from the metal. When you reach the curve in the vein, twist the liner gradually between your thumb and fingers so that its leading point follows the bend. If you must raise the tool before completing a vein be sure to place it back at the exact point from which it was lifted. If you place it too far back, a part of the vein may be more deeply indented than the rest. If you place it too far forward, or to one side, the vein will not be continuous throughout its length and trying to repair the error is a very "chancy" operation. To inscribe the smaller leaf veins, turn the pitch container so the vein you work on will face you lengthwise and then proceed as with the main vein, on its curved portion especially. Here you may use either the straight or curved liner. In using the curved liner hold it so that its curve matches the curve on the leaf.

Once the chasing is done use a medium-sized screwdriver to pry the copper piece out of the pitch. Dig the tool down under the copper, press the handle down and the metal will pop up and out. Try to do this without digging into the piece or distorting its shape. Some pitch

MASTERING BASIC TECHNIQUES

is bound to adhere to the metal. This can be burned off with the torch or disolved with a cloth dipped in kerosene or turpentine, after which it should be washed with soap and water and a stiff bursh. If required, the cleaned metal can be flattened on the bench block with the rawhide hammer. Save the leaf. You will process it further in the following section.

Dapping Metals

Dapping is the process by which metal is formed into domes or hemispheres. It is usually done in conjunction with a dapping die (see jewelry supply catalogs). Since a die is quite an investment, we will substitute the lead block for it. Although the chaser's pitch could be used to support the work, the lead block works better. Use the leaf you made in the previous section to get some idea of what is involved. Place the leaf, chased side down, on the block. Take the largest dapping punch you have (No. 28 or 1 in.) and your utility hammer and begin to strike the punch over the place marked x-1 in Figure 40. Move the punch around the shaded area of x-1 and all the way out past the surrounding edge so as to get a smooth, even, circular surface on the reverse side. The lead will give way under the blows of the hammer and produce a hollow over which the places labeled x-2, x-3, x-4, and x-5 can be dapped in turn. If the depression in the lead gets too deep, you can hammer it down to some degree with your hammer (or use the wider face of the chasing hammer) or you can start in another place on the block.

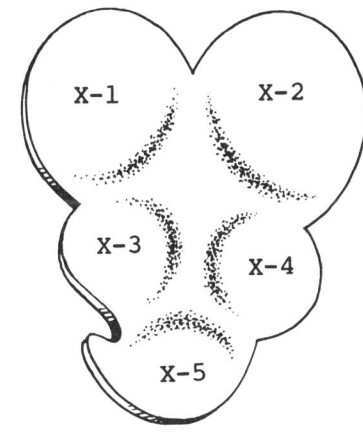

FIGURE 40

This forming process will distort the leaf to some extent. It can be brought back to its original shape with the help of a 4 in. long by ¾ in. square piece of hardwood cut or whittled to a chisel-like (but not too sharp) shape on one end (see A, Fig. 41). Place the leaf, chased side up, on the bench anvil and—using the wooden tool and hammer—follow the leaf's main vein and bump the leaf's mid-portion down about level with the anvil. Do the same between the other dapped areas (arrows in *B,* Figure 41 indicate where and in what direction the makeshift tool should be employed). All the previous dapping and flattening procedures are followed with the No. 22 or ⅞-in., then with the No. 19 or ¾-in. dapping punches to develop an interesting three-dimensional bas-relief aspect to the leaf. *A reminder:* If any high-temperature heating is to be used, this leaf will first have to be carefully brushed with the brass bristle brush to remove all lead particles.

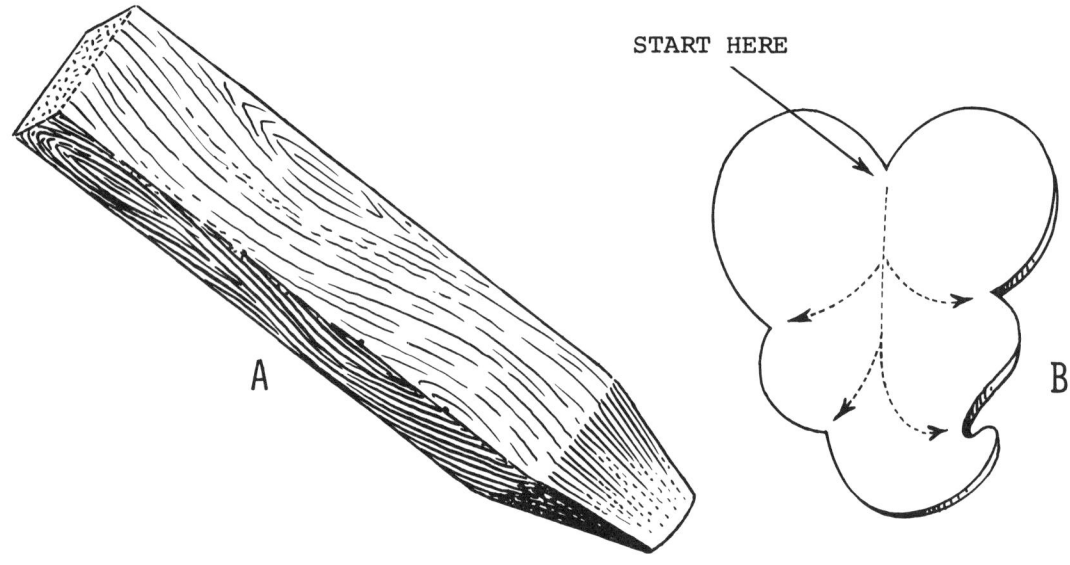

FIGURE 41

REPOUSSÉ

Repoussé (re-poo-say') is similar to dapping, although a much more intricate, decorative technique. Both dapping and repoussé can be done in connection with chasing, and both are usually performed on the opposite side of the metal from that of the chased side. Both are also used to give an article a three-dimensional appearance as opposed to the usual flat and two-dimensional appearance. While repoussé is outside the scope of this book, you ought to have some idea of what it involves. Suppose you wanted to create a face in metal. On the front you would incise or chase such features as the lip line, the eye socket, the outline of the nose, chin, and so on. On the reverse side you would then bump out, or repoussé, the bulge of the lips, the eyebrows and eyeballs, plus the protrusion of the cheeks, chin, nose, and the like.

MASTERING BASIC TECHNIQUES

Annealing Metals

After much hammering, bending, twisting and stretching, all metals tend to lose their qualities of ductility and malleability and become hard and springy. This is a desirable condition in many cases for it enables the metal to maintain the shape given it by the previous work. Besides, there are times when it is desirable for the metal to be springy—in making a tiebar, for example. But this is a desirable condition *only* if no more hammering or other similar forging operation is to be done. More operations cannot be performed on the metal before it is annealed. Annealing is the process used to remove the stress and strain in metal by subjecting it to heat—in other words, to soften it. Unless this is done, further working of the metal will cause it to become brittle and crack. A complicated piece of jewelry that goes through many forming operations may require a number of annealings.

As was said earlier, copper, brass and sterling silver oxidize when heated. Sterling, particularly, under high temperatures develops what is called "fire scale." The scale appears as a dull gray that covers the usually white metal and is hard to remove. This can occur not only in the annealing but also in the hard-soldering process. The gray color is due to the formation of an oxide as the copper in the sterling silver unites with the sulfur in the air. A preventive or at least minimizing step can be taken by preparing a saturated (thick) solution of borax (available in drug and grocery stores and supermarkets) and denatured alcohol (available in hardware and paint stores). Paint the mixture on the metal being annealed or soldered with a small brush or dip the work into the solution. The alcohol burns away under the torch, leaving a thin coating of borax which minimizes or prevents the development of fire scale. Painting silver surfaces with the hard-soldering paste flux that has been recommended will also serve to reduce or eliminate the formation of fire scale. This flux has an added advantage in that it melts (liquefies) at about 1100 degrees. The melting signifies that the appropriate annealing temperature of 1000 to 1200 degrees has been reached.

In the annealing process, the metal is placed on the charcoal block or asbestos pad and a medium-soft flame is applied. (A medium soft flame is one that either does not hiss or hisses only softly as it burns.) Keep the flame moving over the full surface until the metal reaches a dull red color or, if you are using the paste flux, until the flux melts. To see the color, it is well to do the annealing (hard soldering as well) under light that is not too bright. Do not overheat the metal because this causes excessive oxides and scale to form. Once the annealing is done, remove the flame and allow the metal to cool a few seconds until the red color disappears. Then, with your copper tongs, drop the hot metal in the pickle bath and leave it there for several minutes for the pickle to do its work. When the metal appears clean and bright, take it out of the pickle—again with the copper tongs—and wash it in clean water.

A length of wire requires special handling in the annealing process. It should be wound into a small coil that is tightly held together with soft iron binding wire (see Fig. 42). By this means the wire can be heated evenly throughout its length and the danger of melting or burning any part of it is minimized. However, before placing the annealed work in the pickle remove the binding wire, as it can cause a chemical reaction that results in depositing hard-to-get-rid-of black streaks on the metal wherever the binding wire is in contact with it.

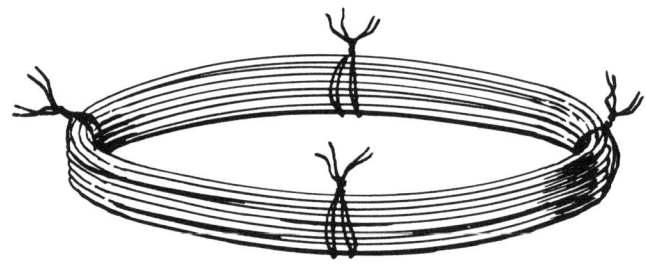

FIGURE 42

Pickling Metals

The purpose in pickling craft metals is to remove the oxides that naturally develop when the metals are exposed to air or heat, and to dissolve the hardened flux that may remain on the metals after hard-soldering operations. Sparex 2 has been recommended since it is a much safer acid than others that are used for pickling. However, it is still an acid and contact with the skin, eyes, mouth, etc., should be avoided. The Sparex comes in a granulated form which, when dissolved in water according to instructions on its container, makes the pickle, or pickle bath. The pickle solution sould be stored in tightly stoppered glass or plastic jars or bottles, with the pickle used for copper and brass kept separate from that used for silver. The copper oxides dissolved by the pickle will eventually turn it a medium shade of blue. When this occurs, the pickle has outlived its usefulness and should be flushed down the drain along with large quantities of water.

Hot metal dropped in heated pickle (it is not advisable to bring the latter to a boil) produces the best and most rapid results. Cold metal placed in hot pickle yields the next most effective results. Cold metal placed in cold pickle will require a long time for the pickle to do its work. The copper tongs should always be used for inserting metal into, and removing metal from, the bath. Hold the metal with the tongs until it has been rinsed in clean water. The metal should then be dried with a clean cloth. If there is doubt as to whether or not all the pickle has been washed away from a piece of jewelry, the article should be boiled in a sodium carbonate-water solution, which will serve to neutralize the acid. A thorough rinsing and drying of the article should follow.

Soldering Metals

It has already been said that there are two types of soldering employed in jewelry making—soft soldering, which is used to a limited degree, and hard soldering, which is employed wherever feasible. There are basic rules, however, which apply to both types of soldering if metals are to be joined successfully.

1. The surfaces to be joined must fit as closely together as possible. Hard solder will not bridge gaps between metal surfaces. Lead solder will to a limited extent, but the result is usually a sloppy, amateurish-looking join.

MASTERING BASIC TECHNIQUES

2. The surfaces to be joined must be absolutely clean. No solder—soft or hard—will flow onto or over metal surfaces contaminated with oxides, dust, grease, wax or oil (including that from human hands). Instead, the solder will roll itself into a ball and stubbornly refuse to move until the surfaces, including its own, are suitably clean. There are several different ways for ensuring the cleanliness of metal for soldering:

    a. Scrub the surfaces with a stiff bristle brush and a detergent-water solution into which a little household ammonia has been mixed. Follow this by a rinse in clean water—first hot, then cold—and dry with a clean, lint-free cloth.

    b. Sand the surfaces to be joined and those bordering on them with a *clean* piece of fine sanding cloth. In all cases avoid touching these same surfaces with your hands or fingers after they have been cleaned. Use a tweezer to move them about or handle them by edges not to be involved in the joining process.

    c. Annealing the metal in the manner previously described will burn away wax, grease and oil. Pickling the metal in a hot pickle bath will remove the oxides. Follow this with a good scrubbing with the above detergent-ammonia-water solution and then dry with a proper cloth. This will definitely ensure metal surfaces appropriately prepared for soldering.

SOFT SOLDERING

This form of soldering is quite easy to do. The projects will help you to understand where its use is acceptable in jewelry making. Soft solder in wire form has been recommended, but you should not apply the wire to the heated part as plumbers do in soldering copper pipe, because the main problem with soft soldering is to use just enough to unite the parts and no more. Instead, hammer the wire thin and flat on the bench anvil, then cut small pieces from this with cutting pliers as it is needed. In the soft-soldering process it is wise to apply less solder to the join than you think is needed because, first, it is easy to apply more if required, and, second, it is extra work to remove the excess. In addition to fitting pieces to be joined as closely as possible and cleaning the surfaces to be joined by one of the methods prescribed above, the basic procedures of soft soldering are:

1. Apply liquid soft soldering flux to the surfaces to be joined.

2. With a tweezer, place the right amounts of solder in the right places. This will vary as the shape of the parts to be united will vary and more will be said about this when we come to the projects.

3. Employ a soft flame for soft soldering and heat the entire piece first by moving the torch over the full area of the metal. Solder—both soft and hard—flows toward the spot where the metal is hottest. The moment you see the solder start to melt, aim your torch at the solder and direct its flow exactly to where you want it. By judicious use of the torch you can lead the solder down a long seam to the precise area in which you want it to settle. As soon as this is done remove the flame and wait until the solder cools ("freezes") before moving the parts you have joined. If the amount of solder used was not enough to make a solid join and the metal surfaces are still clean, reflux the spots involved, place more solder where needed and reheat the article until the solder flows. If too much solder was used, the excess

should be removed with the hollow scraper or later it will interfere with the coloring of the metal. On copper and brass it will obviously show up as a blemish.

HARD SOLDERING

This type of soldering is much more difficult to do properly than is soft soldering. With patience, practice and perseverance, however, the beginner can master the technique. The first step is to prepare the solder. Clean the surfaces of a sheet of hard solder with fine sanding cloth, than use your rule to draw lines (see Fig. 43) that are about 1/32 in. apart and at right angles to each other. Hold the solder over a clean sheet of paper and use your plate shears to cut the sheet into small squares. Make your first cut by fringing the sheet lengthwise to a distance of about 1 inch, then make the cut at right angles to this fringe. To keep the small pieces—also referred to as "snippets" or *paillons* (pie-yons')—from flying away during the right-angle cutting, place the index finger of one hand along the line of *paillons* being cut so that the latter strike the finger and drop onto the paper. Some craftsmen cut the snippets of solder as they need them; others cut the entire sheet at one time. If you follow the first course, each grade of solder should be marked with your scriber—*E* for Easy, *M* for Medium, and *H* for Hard. If you follow the second course, each grade of solder should have a separate labeled container so that solder with different melting points will not be mixed.

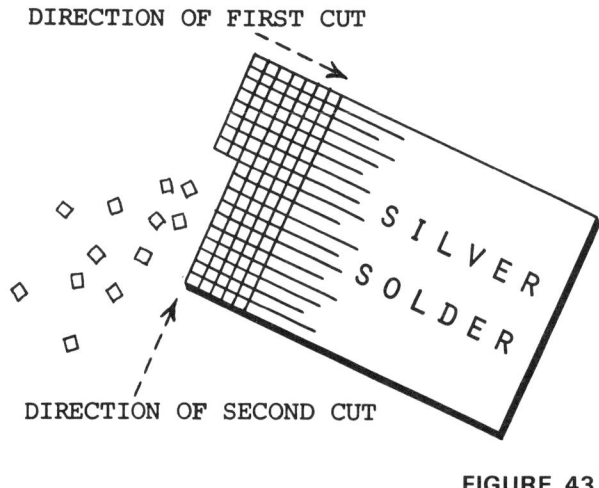

FIGURE 43

The steps to be followed for hard soldering are fundamentally the same as for soft soldering with some additions and a few exceptions. The close fitting of surfaces to be joined is essential in hard soldering since—unlike soft solder which flows between surfaces and basically "glues" them together—hard solder flows between surfaces and melts just enough of their

MASTERING BASIC TECHNIQUES

outer layers as to "weld" them together. Obviously the surfaces to be joined must be in close contact with each other.

The removal of even thin coats of oil, grease, wax and oxides is mandatory in hard soldering. Hard solder is much more finicky than soft solder. It absolutely will not flow on surfaces that are not bright and clean. Paste flux is recommended for hard soldering. This paste is applied with a small, clean brush to the areas to be joined. The paste has a water base, and after standing a while water may rise to the top, making the upper part of the flux quite thin. In this event, stir the flux with a suitable clean implement (spatula) to bring it back to a creamy consistency.

For practice, cut two pieces of copper and two of brass, each ½ in. square and of the same gauge. The pieces must be filed absolutely square, with their edges perpendicular to the top and bottom surfaces. Make sure they are perfectly flat by striking them on the bench anvil with flat-faced blows of your rawhide hammer. Line them up as shown in Fig. 44 and make sure that the edges which butt together fit closely along their entire length. If not, file them until they do. Place a few snippets of Hard-grade solder in a small dish or on a clean piece of paper. Place the top squares of copper and brass on your charcoal block or asbestos pad, making certain they lie flat. Flux the top surface of both squares, including the butting edges. One commonly used method for putting solder in the proper place—in this case along the butt join—is to pick up and transport a snippet with the tip of a flux-moistened brush. Place three pieces on the juncture about ⅛ in. apart.

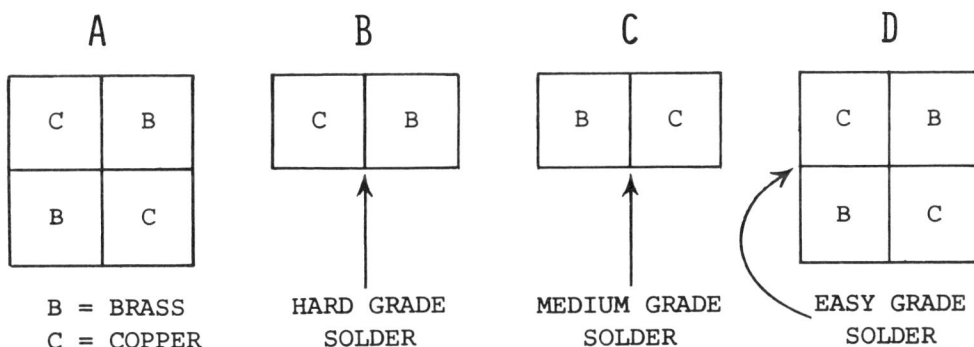

FIGURE 44

The amount of heat needed to make the solder flow decreases somewhat as the hardness of the solder used decreases. Some cardinal rules in all soldering processes are:

1. Heat the metal as quickly as possible, but only enough to cause the solder to flow.

2. Avoid excessive heat, because this may produce fire scale (on silver) as well as more oxides than the flux can absorb and thus keep the solder from flowing.

3. Use a medium-sized flame which does not hiss loudly and which has some yellow or

orange color rather than being all blue. Note, too, that the hottest part of the flame is the section just about midway between the blue cone that appears at the point of the torch and the tip of the flame.

Use a soft flame to evaporate the water from the flux and be sure to keep the flame moving. As the water boils away, the solder may jump around and, possibly, move out of place. If necessary, push it back in place with your tweezer or pusher (see below), making sure that the copper and brass are still butted tightly together. As soon as the flux melts, increase the flame to a medium size and keep it moving. Watch the solder carefully and, when it begins to melt, center the flame on the join and draw the solder along so that it flows the full length of the join. Remember that solder flows to the hottest part of the metal; so that heating the metal just ahead of the flowing solder will attract it in the direction you want it to go. Now, return the Hard-grade solder to its container and put some snippets of Medium-grade solder on the dish or paper. Repeat the previous operation with this grade of solder, joining the two free squares of brass and copper. Then repeat the procedure and join the two rectangles you have assembled, this time using Easy-grade solder. Between each soldering operation, it may be necessary to pickle the metal to remove the oxides that have formed. Pickling definitely will be necessary after the last soldering.

At this point, it is worth mentioning a "make-it-yourself" tool that some craftsmen use in the hard-soldering process. It is called a "pusher" and is made from a 6-in. piece of steel rod $\frac{1}{8}$ in. in diameter, one-third of which is filed to a long slender point. The rod is available in some hardware stores and from many jewelry supply companies. The pusher can be used to move solder back into place during a soldering operation, and to transport solder to the spot where it is needed to unite metal parts. In the latter case, a snippet of solder is placed on the asbestos pad and heated. As the solder draws itself up into a ball, the pusher's point is put in contact with the ball and heat is applied until the solder sticks to the tool. The heat is then moved to the fluxed jewelry parts to be joined, with the solder ball held above the flame to keep it hot. Once the flux melts, the ball is placed on the juncture of the parts to be joined with the flame more or less centered on that particular area. In a short time, the solder will flow from the pusher to the join.

Before leaving the subject of soldering, a word should also be said about the role yellow ochre can play in the hard-soldering operation, especially in those instances where more than one grade of solder is used in successive soldering steps. In a complicated piece which includes sheet metal, wires in various forms, plus other shapes that are being soldered together, there is always the possibility that the heat from the current soldering step will melt the solder used in previous steps and cause the piece to come apart. This can be prevented to a great degree by the use of yellow ochre which is mixed in water to a creamy paste and painted on the previously soldered join or joins with a small camel's hair brush. The yellow ochre—also known as an anti-flux or anti-solder—prevents the solder from melting and flowing. It is important to keep the ochre away from the new join being soldered, as otherwise no soldering will take place. It is also important to scrub the ochre from the article before pickling it because the ochre will discolor and contaminate the pickle. Other anti-solders are

MASTERING BASIC TECHNIQUES

powdered jeweler's rouge and powdered asbestos, both prepared and applied in the same way as the ochre.

Smoothing Metals

Metal smoothing is concerned with the removal of nicks, pits, scratches and other blemishes present when you received the metal or put there as you worked with it. The smoothing process involves the use of files, sanding cloth, and the Scotch stone, in that order. It is difficult to tell exactly which file or grade of cloth to start with because that depends on the extent and nature of the blemish. A good rule of thumb is to start with the *coarsest* file or cloth that will, in your judgment, eliminate most of the blemish. For example, no time or effort is saved in trying to remove deep scratches with a fine grade of sanding cloth. Another rule of thumb is to progress in succession from the coarsest file or cloth through each finer cut of file and grade of cloth until you get to the Scotch stone. In that way the marks left by the preceding tool or material will be eradicated by the one which follows.

The main problem in getting rid of a blemish on metal is to avoid leaving a depression or valley where the blemish has been. In filing or sanding a dent or deep scratch, for instance, file or sand across the length and breadth so as to remove some metal around the marks. Folding the abrasive cloths around a block of wood or wood dowel of suitable size will also help to avoid the development of a valley in the small area formerly occupied by the blemish. The scratches left by the finest grade of sanding cloth can be removed by the Scotch stone. The stone, being softer than any craft metal, will wear away and leave a muddy residue on the metal. Occasionally wash away this mud in order to observe the progress you are making. This brings up a third rule of thumb: Do not fool yourself into thinking that the polishing compounds will make blemishes disappear. They may, on some occasions, but only after hours of hard work. The fact is that with most metals the higher the polish the more the disfiguring marks will stand out. When that happens, it is usually back to the files, abrasive cloths and Scotch stone.

The steel burnisher can be classified as both a smoothing and a polishing tool because it can be used for either purpose providing it is kept highly polished and free from rust, nicks, and scratches. To prevent rust, it should be lightly oiled between each use. Small pits, scratches and similar imperfections can be removed from metal surfaces with the burnisher by vigorously rubbing the affected area in a more or less circular motion. This motion has the effect of moving the relatively soft surface of the metal until the disfigurements are erased. The metal must, of course, be supported from underneath so that it will not be warped or bent out of shape. This support can be provided by your fingers or by the end of a dapping punch or hammer—whatever fits the underside best—secured in the bench vise. Some craftsmen burnish (texture) all of the jewelry piece that the burnisher can reach, leaving the surface covered with a series of gleaming swirls that are more appealing, in their eyes, then the uniform polish imparted by the tripoli and rouge polishing compounds.

Polishing and Coloring Metals

POLISHING

Polishing, so far as this book is concerned, is the process whereby marks left by the fine sanding cloths and Scotch stone are eliminated from the metal, leaving gleaming, lustrous surfaces. For reasons discussed earlier, this book limits the polishing process to hand polishing. Such polishing was performed with excellent results long before motors were invented. And, truth to tell, if marring the metal has been avoided during the construction process or if blemishes were removed in the smoothing process, then a high polish can be easily achieved by hand.

The two compounds most often used for polishing craft metals are, first, tripoli and, second, jeweler's rouge. Once the smoothing process is completed, the work should be washed out with hot water, detergent or soap, and a bristle brush to remove any abrasive dust, wax, grease or oil that may be on the metal. Rinse the article thoroughly and dry it with a clean cloth or paper towel. (Make certain it is completely dry, as otherwise the tripoli compound will cling to the metal and be hard to remove.) Next, rub some tripoli compound on your felt buffing stick and apply this with long strokes and a reasonable amount of pressure over the surface of the work. The tripoli compound consists of a very fine abrasive imbedded in wax, so do not apply too much at one time or the wax will build up on the buffer and delay the polishing process. When you have polished the article to your satisfaction, wash and dry it as before. Then, while holding it by its edges, examine it closely to make sure that all unsightly marks have been eliminated and that all the tripoli compound has been washed away.

It is at this point that fire scale, if any, on the surfaces of the work will reveal itself. The evidence is blobs of grayish-black which, unless removed, will tarnish darker than the other parts of the metal. This is not too bad on the back of the jewelry, but it is terribly ugly on the front where it can be seen, particularly if it is in an area that is to be left highly polished. If you find fire scale, you must first pickle, wash and dry the article. Then sand it with fine sanding cloth, use the Scotch stone, wash and dry, and, finally, apply tripoli compound as before. Wash and dry again to see if you have gotten rid of the fire scale. If not, then the entire process must be repeated again and as many times as necessary. The elimination of fire scale is a tedious process, but if it is not removed it can spoil the appearance of an otherwise attractive piece of work. That is why it is so important never to use excessive heat on the metal. In the annealing and hard-soldering procedures, the metal should never be heated beyond a dull red color. Perform these processes in a dim light, as was stated earlier, so that you clearly observe when the metal has reached the proper color.

The second step in the polishing process—whether or not you antique the jewelry—is the application of jeweler's rouge. This compound is applied with the chamois polishing buff reserved for it and it alone. Jeweler's rouge does not contain an abrasive, but imparts a high, sparkling polish to surfaces previously buffed with tripoli compound. After you have rouged the jewelry article to your satisfaction, wash the item as before and dry it carefully with a clean, soft (cotton flannel, if available) cloth.

MASTERING BASIC TECHNIQUES

COLORING

The next step is usually the coloring or deliberate oxidation (antiquing) of the jewelry. Coloring is largely a matter of personal taste. Some craftsmen prefer to omit the coloring step with certain articles of jewelry and to leave the pieces with only the polish produced by tripoli compound or by tripoli compound followed by jeweler's rouge. The purpose of antiquing is to give the article more character and more of a three-dimensional aspect than it would have by just being highly polished. Copper and silver can be antiqued with potassium sulfide (a chemical also known as "liver of sulfur") which is available from chemical and jewelry supply houses and from most local pharmacies. *Warning:* This substance smells like rotten eggs and must be stored in a dark container in a dark place, as it deteriorates very quickly in the presence of air and light.

Dissolve a half-inch cube in a pint of very hot water in which the article to be oxidized—having been thoroughly cleaned—is immersed. Watch the color and remove the item with your copper tongs once it has turned to the color you want—a grayish black or black, depending on your taste. Then rinse the item to stop the oxidation process. Do not make the solution too strong or allow the article to remain in it so long that the oxide on the jewelry becomes thick and flakes off in places. If this happens, it means the piece must be buffed with tripoli compound, cleaned again and the oxidation process repeated.

The antiquing of brass is accomplished in the same way except that antimony trichloride ("butter of antimony") is used in place of the liver of sulfur. This substance also is available from chemical supply houses or a local pharmacy. Put three to four teaspoonfuls in a cup of hot water and immerse the jewelry in the solution. The same precautions as to the strength of the solution and the time the jewelry is immersed therein are taken with this chemical as with the potassium sulfide.

The coloring process is essentially a speeding up of what would normally occur to the jewelry with the passage of time. Copper, brass and silver oxidize over a period of time. As the article is worn in the form of jewelry, it rubs against clothing and against the wearer's body, with the result that the high spots of the jewelry piece are kept free of oxide while the low spots gradually turn a grayish black or black. You achieve the same effect in much less time by highlighting the high areas of your jewelry using tripoli compound with the hand buff, while leaving the low areas oxidized. This applies to the back of the article as well as to the front. Once you are satisfied with the effect, wash the article, and make sure that all the tripoli compound is removed. A good way to do this is to boil the article in an enamelled or heat-proof-glass pot in water with detergent or soap and a little ammonia solution. Then rinse thoroughly and dry. There are other surface treatments that can be given to jewelry, and these will be discussed as they are come to in the projects.

Although the creation of jewelry of your own design should be your ultimate goal, your efforts in that direction will not succeed unless you become fully familiar with the metals, the tools and the basic processes. Therefore, practice the processes to the point where they become a kind of second nature to you. In doing so, you free your mind for the envisioning and inventing it must do in your search for the new, the novel, the original. The chapters which follow ask you, by and large, to copy jewelry made by someone else. If all they do is to teach you to imitate the work of another person, they will have failed in their purpose. Their main intent is to provide you with the experience you will need for fashioning articles of jewelry born of your own imagination and creativity.

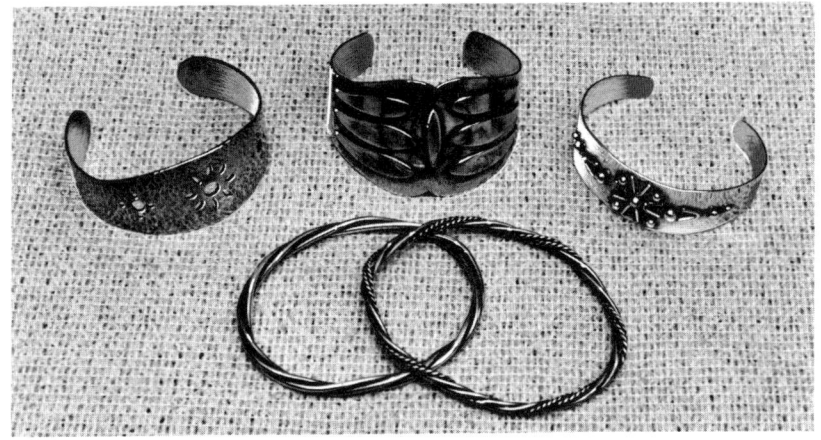

FIGURE 45

4/BRACELETS

The first three projects consist of the open-end bracelets shown in Figure 45. Open-end bracelets were chosen as the introductory work because this type can easily be made to fit most wrists merely by increasing or decreasing the distance between the ends.

PROJECT 1: Copper Open-End Bracelet

Although the first piece of jewelry to be worked on is an open-end copper bracelet, the same article could be made out of brass or silver. Copper was selected because it is fairly inexpensive and, if a piece is spoiled, it can be put aside so as to salvage what you can from it for another project.

Begin by cutting a piece of 16-ga. copper 6 in. long by 1⅛ in. wide. Flatten the piece on the bench anvil with the rawhide mallet. Now is the time to get rid of any bad nicks or scratches in the area which the bracelet itself will occupy and particularly the surface you intend to make its top surface. Minor blemishes may be disregarded at this stage. Use files, sanding cloth and Scotch stone as needed. When you have finished, make sure that all the metal filings and abrasive grit are removed from the metal. Place the copper on the bench anvil and, with moderate blows, strike the top surface with one end of your embossing hammer to produce small indentations. Overlap these indentations so as not to leave any flat spots anywhere on the metal's surface. The metal has a tendency to curl up during this process and should be flattened with the rawhide mallet when necessary. The purpose of this process is to texture the copper's surface and to harden the copper so that it will not lose its shape once it is bent to form a bracelet.

The design for this bracelet was transferred to the copper by drawing it on paper (you can trace the drawing in Fig. 46), carefully cutting out the bracelet's outline from the pattern and then gluing this to the textured surface of the metal. You can use this method or any of those given earlier for transferring designs. The dots in the circles and ovals represent points where the metal should be center-punched. Do this right through the paper; also drill through the paper, supporting the work by one of the methods described in Chapter 3. The large circle in the middle of the center design is made with a No. 23 (5/32 in.) bit, while the two next smaller circles are drilled with a No. 42 (3/32 in.) bit. The smallest circles are drilled with a No. 53 (1/16 in.) bit. This same bit is used to cut openings in the ovals through which a No. 3/0 saw blade is threaded so that the ovals can be pierced. Try to make the openings as uniform as possible. Use the side of the blade's teeth to smooth the walls of the piercings.

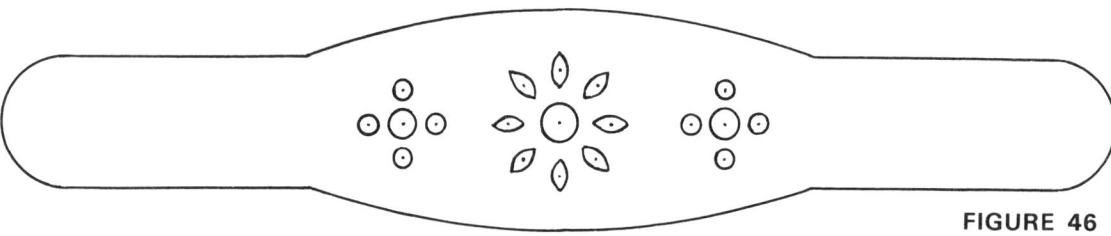

FIGURE 46

Before cutting out the bracelet's shape, eliminate the burrs, if any, caused by the drilling. Support the copper piece on the V-block and cut out the shape of the bracelet using a No. 2/0 saw blade. Remove the paper pattern and file and smooth the edges all around. The method for removing the paper—peeling it off, washing or burning it off—will depend on the type of adhesive which was used in affixing the pattern to the metal. If you burn the paper off be sure not to overheat the metal and thus soften it. If you removed the blemishes from the top surface before texturing and handled the metal carefully during the drilling and piercing operations, there should be, hopefully, little or no need for the further smoothing of this side. Hopefully, because much smoothing will tend to eradicate the texture you put on. Before proceeding to smooth the bracelet's underside, you should protect the textured side by covering it with masking tape.

The next step is to bend the metal to a bracelet shape. First, remove the masking tape from the top side of the metal. Center the piece lengthwise across the mandrel and, with your hands, begin to press the metal around it, starting from the center and working out toward the ends. If you have any difficulty in getting the bracelet's ends to lie flat at all points gently stroke the metal down with your mallet. Start your strokes from a point just beyond that at which the copper stands away from the mandrel and hammer toward the

BRACELETS

ends. If necessary, use your hands to do the final rounding with the bracelet off the mandrel. Also press or pull the ends until they are about 1¼ in. to 1½ in. apart, depending upon the size of the wrist for which the bracelet is intended. Do this gently so as not to put a sharp bend in any part of the metal. You will find that a sharp bend in metal can be difficult, if not impossible, to remove.

Next, you will need the tripoli compound and felt polishing stick. Rub the stick's felt side across the bar several times to pick up a fair amount of compound. While supporting the bracelet with one hand apply the tripoli to the metal with long strokes and a reasonable amount of pressure. Work along the long axis of the bracelet and mainly in the same direction. Check on your progress by occasionally washing the article in warm soapy water with a bit of ammonia and using a soft bristle brush. Rinse and dry with a soft, clean cloth. Continue the operation until the marks left by the smoothing process are gone from all surfaces of the bracelet. Then wash, rinse and dry the metal, making certain that all the wax left by the tripoli compound has been cleaned away, including the surfaces inside the holes and piercings.

While antiquing a bracelet of this type is not mandatory, adding a bit of color to the copper does help to reduce its shiny newness so that it will not look as if it has been stamped out by a machine. Prepare the hot liver of sulfur solution according to the instructions given earlier and place the bracelet in the solution until it turns black or grayish black. Remove it, rinse to stop the oxidizing action and dry it thoroughly. Apply tripoli compound as before, but rub rather lightly so as not to take out all the black in the top surface's depressions. Do the same on the underside of the article. The edges of the bracelet will look better if they are bright. Do not be concerned if some parts of the bracelet's large surfaces retain more oxidation than others. This, in the opinion of many craftsmen, lends individuality to the jewelry. Now you face a decision. Some craftsmen prefer the soft glow on metal left by the tripoli compound to the brighter gleam produced by the rouge. It is a matter of personal taste. Should you opt for the higher polish, apply jeweler's rouge with the chamois polishing stick, using the same procedure you employed with the tripoli. Wash the article once you are satisfied with the result.

Copper tarnishes rather quickly unless given a protective coat of clear metal lacquer. The problem with lacquer, however, is that it can be rather easily chipped or scratched. When this occurs, the places no longer protected by lacquer will tarnish, producing ugly black streaks and blotches on the metal. Getting rid of these streaks will entail dissolving the lacquer from the entire piece with the aid of lacquer thinner, washing and repolishing the article and, possibly, relacquering. it. There is an alternative, however. The piece can be left unlacquered and, upon tarnishing, can be repolished by using tripoli and rouge as before, or by using a commercial polishing liquid sold in most supermarkets and hardware stores. Thus, you are faced with another decision.

If you decide to lacquer the bracelet, first make sure that it is perfectly clean and free from dust and lint. Handle the piece by the edges. In a suitable clean container place a mixture of two parts lacquer and one part lacquer thinner. Mix enough to cover the entire bracelet when it is dipped in the liquid. Cut a 10-in. length of your thinnest binding wire, straighten it and bend up about 1½ in. to 2 in. of one end to form a round hook. Suspend the article from this wire by threading the hook through one of the holes in the design. Holding the free end of the wire, dip the bracelet into the thinned lacquer, making certain that all the surfaces are covered by the liquid. Take the piece out and hold it over the container to allow the excess lacquer to run off. Shaking the piece gently will help to remove the excess. Should any stubborn blobs of lacquer remain on the piece, brush them out with a clean soft brush. Work fast because lacquer dries quickly. Hang the bracelet by the wire in a dust-free place where it will not come in contact with anything else and let it dry for about an hour. Make sure that the wire is not touching any part of the wide surfaces of the piece because this will leave a mark in the lacquer. The thinned lacquer can be saved and used again by storing it in an airtight container. Do not pour it back into its original container. Should it thicken in time, it can be restored to the proper consistency by adding a little thinner.

What have you accomplished in this project? First, you have taken a raw piece of shapeless metal and created an item attractive to the eye. Second, you have created something about which you can say, "I made this with my own two hands!" Third, you have had practice in a number of metalworking techniques: sawing, drilling, smoothing, forming, coloring and polishing. And fourth, you are better prepared to move on to your next project.

PROJECT 2: Brass/Copper Open-End Bracelet

The base portion for this open-end bracelet (labeled *B,* in Fig. 47) is cut from 16-ga. brass. The decorative segments (labeled *C*) are made from 20-ga. copper, and making them is the first step in this project. Start by reproducing the design on paper or by tracing it on tracing paper. Next, cut a piece of 20-ga. copper 3 in. long by 1½ in. wide and clean one side of it thoroughly. Apply white tempera paint to this surface and let it dry. Then transfer the outlines of the decorative copper segments onto the tempera-coated metal by one of the suggested transfer methods. With your scriber carefully but lightly scratch these out-

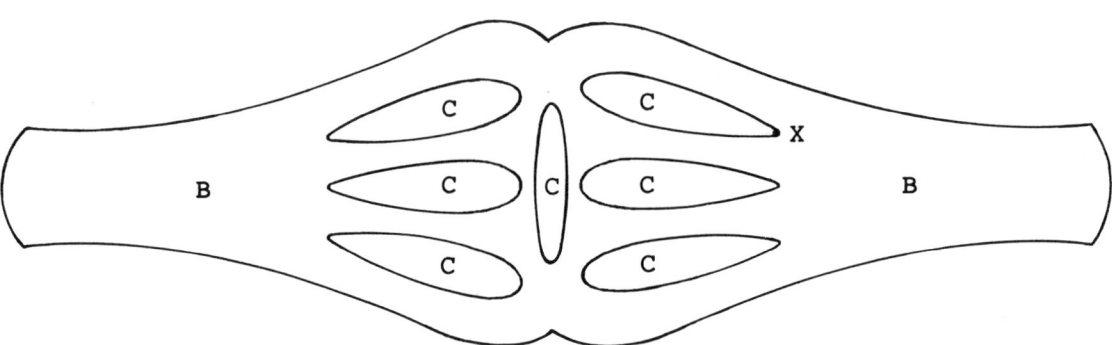

FIGURE 47

BRACELETS

lines through the paint and onto the copper. Wash away the paint, dry the metal and saw out the segments with a No. 3/0 blade. Saw outside the line so as to leave some excess metal for filing and sanding.

Next, cut out the outline of the brass portion of the bracelet. Cut a piece of 16-ga. brass 6 in. long by 1¾ in. wide and glue the paper pattern to the brass. Saw out the bracelet with a No. 2/0 blade. File and smooth the edges, rounding them slightly so that they will not cut the wearer's wrist. The knife-shaped needle file is best for filing that part of the center portion that curves inward and comes together in a sharp inside point. Note the little dot labeled X on the top, right copper decoration in Fig. 47. This X indicates that you are to use your scriber to prick through the paper to produce a tiny indentation on the surface of the brass not only at this point but at several points around the outline of each copper decoration shown. These indentations will mark the places on the brass where the copper pieces are to be soldered. Pushing down on the scriber as you twirl it between your thumb and first two fingers will produce the marks required. Remove the paper pattern.

Since there will be areas on the brass that will be difficult to reach with files and sanding cloth once the copper pieces are soldered, now is the time to remove any blemishes. Some craftsmen often go as far as the tripoli polishing stage before soldering the parts together. The tripoli compound must, of course, be washed from the parts before the soldering operation.

This project introduces a technique not prevously discussed, called appliqué (ap-lih-kay'). This technique consists of soldering a piece or pieces of metal onto, usually, a larger piece of metal to produce a three-dimensional effect. In our present project soft solder will be used to join the copper pieces to the brass so that you can become acquainted with this solder. Make sure that the copper cutouts lie flat on the bench anvil, then clean the surfaces that are to receive the solder. Take a 6 in. length of soft solder wire and hammer one end (about 1½ in.) as flat and as thin as possible. Cut off small sections of this with the cutting pliers. Place one copper piece on the asbestos pad, apply flux and set two or three pieces of solder on the copper. Use a small, soft flame to melt the solder. Use more solder if needed to cover the entire surface of the metal but use as little as possible to accomplish this. Move the melted solder with a flux-filled brush to help distribute it in a thin, even coat. Keep the flame away while doing this so as not to burn up the brush. Apply solder to all the copper pieces, using these same procedures.

Place the brass portion of the bracelet (it must be absolutely clean) on the charcoal block, marked surface up. Apply the flux to one of the places assigned to a copper segment, then position a matching copper piece in this space, soldered side down. Use a soft flame until a bright, silvery line appears all around the copper's bottom edge indicating that the solder has flowed. Allow the solder to freeze, then repeat the various steps with the remaining copper parts. If thin solder coats were applied to these parts, no solder should be markedly visible on the brass.

Pickle, clean, smooth and polish the bracelet surfaces as required. Bend the bracelet to shape, using the same techniques as for the previous copper bracelet. Color the bracelet with antimony trichloride according to instructions given earlier. Clean, dry and polish with jeweler's rouge. If you desire, you may apply a coat of lacquer to the bracelet, but, if you do, you must be certain that the wire used to hold the bracelet holds it by its edges and not by any of its broad surfaces. For our next project, we will do a bracelet in sterling silver.

PROJECT 3: Sterling Silver Open-End Bracelet

The main part of this bracelet is 18-ga. silver sheet, 6 in. long by ¾ in. wide at the widest part. The bracelet tapers to ½ in. at the rounded ends. Your first step in making this bracelet will be to reproduce the design (see Fig. 48) and transfer it to the metal. The easiest way to do this is to trace the design on paper and then glue the paper to the metal. Use your scriber as before to prick through the paper to mark the position of the applied V's and the silver beads which are indicated by the little blackened circles. For marking the positions of the beads place the scriber as near to the center of each circle as pos-

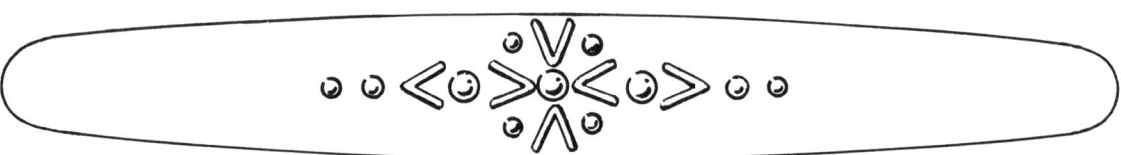

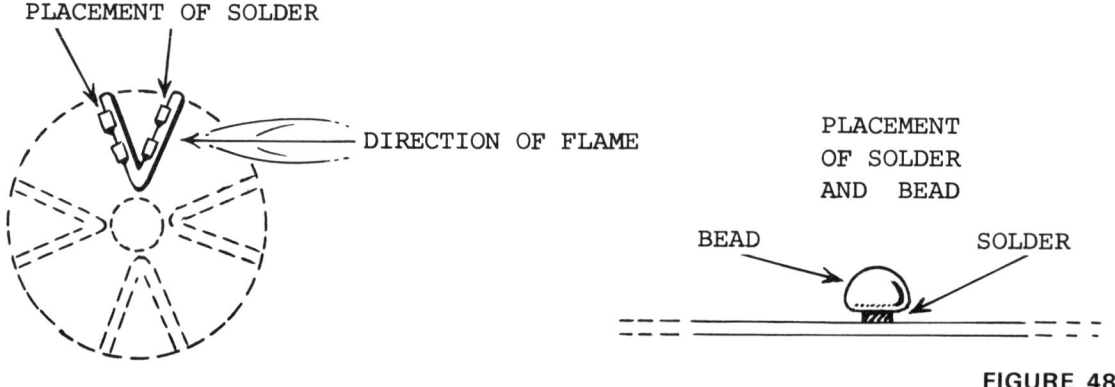

FIGURE 48

sible. The method of making these beads will be described shortly. But, for now, cut out the outline of the bracelet, clean and smooth its surface and set it aside. *Note:* If craft metal is to be put aside for any length of time, it is best placed in a clean container and covered with clean water so that dust, grease and sulfur in the air cannot reach it.

BRACELETS

The six V's—all the same size—are made from 9/16-in. lengths of 18-ga. silver wire. File the ends flat to remove the chisel-like points left by the cutting pliers. With the scriber lightly mark the exact midpoint on each V and use your forming pliers to bend the length of silver wire into a V-shape that will match those in Fig. 48. Note where the Easy-grade hard-solder snippets are to be placed in soldering the V's to the bracelet part. The V's should be pickled first and handled thereafter only with the tweezers. A good procedure is to lightly flux the spot where a V is to be placed, then dry the flux with a soft flame. Next, position a lightly fluxed V in place and again dry the flux. Then set the solder snippets so that they touch the bracelet's base while leaning against the V. In soldering smaller pieces such as the V's to a larger piece such as the main part of the bracelet, it is important to bring the temperature *of the large piece* up to the temperature at which the solder will flow, otherwise the solder will run up on the wires and no joining will occur. Heat the metal with a moderate flame, noting the direction from which to heat the metals being joined once the solder starts to flow. Keep the pusher handy to reset any solder snippets or V's that may shift out of place. All the V's may be soldered at one time provided you are careful to see that nothing moves out of position in the process. Pickle the work as often as is necessary to remove the oxides and hardened flux.

Making metal beads is a simple process. The center bead, the largest on the bracelet, is made by placing a ⅞-in. piece of 18-ga. silver wire on the charcoal block and then heating it. It will soon turn red hot, begin to curl in on itself and finally form itself into a bead (actually a half bead), after which you should remove the heat. With the copper tongs drop the bead into the pickle once it has lost its red glow. The next smaller beads (six are required) are similarly made form ¾-in. lengths of 18-ga. silver wire, while the smallest beads (two are needed) are produced from ⅝-in., 18-ga. wire.

Metal beads of the same size can be made from scrap silver of any gauge if you have a balance scale available. For example: You would make one bead out of a ¾-in. piece of 18-ga. wire. This bead is then placed in one pan of the scale and scrap metal is placed in the other pan until the two are in exact balance. The scrap is then placed on the charcoal block and melted down to form a bead. Any number of beads of a particular size can be made by this method. Copper or brass wire and scrap can also be used to form beads in the same manner.

Figure 48 illustrates one way of soldering a bead to the bracelet. First, the place for the bead is lightly fluxed and the flux dried. Next, a snippet of solder is placed on the exact spot where the bead should be centered (after being pickled and rinsed), and the appropriate bead, its bottom surface fluxed, is placed so as to rest on the solder. The bracelet is then heated —slowly at first so as not to dislodge the solder or bead—and then with a hotter flame until the solder flows. This flow is indicated by the bead's suddenly settling down to the metal surface. The other bead-soldering method is to first produce a small indentation in the charcoal block with the ball end of the chasing hammer or the smallest dapping punch. Set the bead in this indentation, top down. Place a little flux on the flat bottom of the bead along with a snippet of Easy-grade solder, then heat the bead until the solder flows. After pickling, rinsing and drying, position the bead on the fluxed spot where it belongs and solder it on by reheating until the solder flows. Keep your pusher handy to reposition any bead that is moved out of place.

When all the parts have been soldered on and the bracelet pickled for the last time, follow the steps for smoothing, bending, coloring and polishing the bracelet outlined in the first two projects.

Women have long favored the narrow bracelets, called "bangle" bracelets, as arm ornaments. So, as our next project, we will make one. The inclusion of this type of bracelet provides an opportunity to familiarize you with the technique of twisting craft metal wires for decorative effects.

PROJECT 4: Copper/Silver Bangle Bracelet

This bracelet consists of two strands of copper wire and one of silver; all wire being 12-ga. wire and 10 in. long. First, each wire should be wound into a small coil that is tied with thin binding wire (as was shown in Fig. 42) and annealed. The ends of the binding wire are twisted fairly tight with the flat-nosed pliers. Follow the annealing instructions given in Chapter 3, being careful not to overheat any part of the wire and thus melt it. Pickle the coils, but be sure to remove the binding wire before placing them in the bath. Rinse and dry them, then straighten the wires as much as possible with your hands, line them up in the order shown in Figure 49 and tighten about ½ in. of them in the *unshielded* jaws of your bench vise. Pull the wires taut (there should be no gaps between them) by clamping their other ends in your hand vise and twist them clockwise about five or six full turns, exerting an even pull at all times during the process.

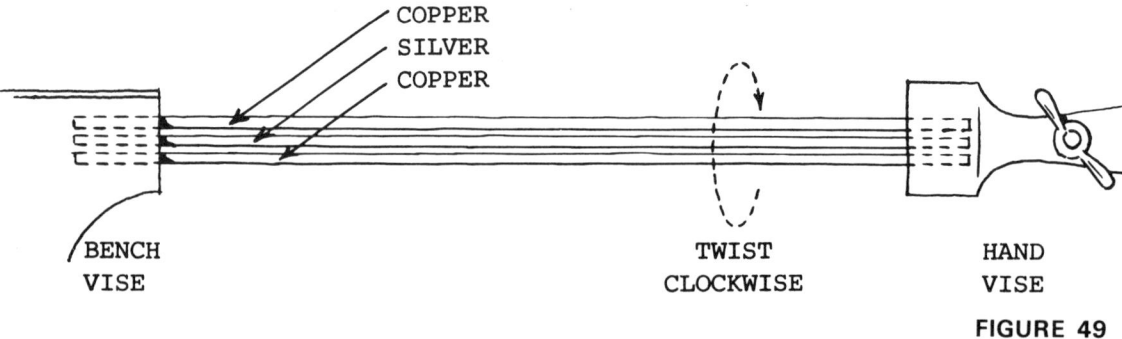

FIGURE 49

Remove the wires from the hand vise. Pulling and twisting will have made the wires fairly stiff and reduced their length about ½ in. Another ½ in. on each end will have been damaged by the jaws of the vises. Thus, you will end up with a bracelet about 8½ in. in circumference, which is plenty large enough to fit over the average woman's hand. Now saw off the

BRACELETS

damaged part still held in the bench vise, using the jeweler's saw and a No. 2/0 blade (save the damaged silver wire scrap). Insert the other end of the wires in the bench vise and repeat the process.

To keep the ends of the wires from springing apart when formed into a circle, solder them to each other at each end with Medium-grade solder. File the ends so that they are perfectly flat and perpendicular to their circumference. Bend the wires around your bracelet mandrel so the ends overlap each other by about ¼ in. Do not be concerned if the bracelet is not perfectly round; you will have a chance to round it later. Remove the bracelet from the mandrel and, by pulling and twisting it with your hands, work to get the ends to spring together as squarely as possible. Push the ends down toward the bracelet center, if necessary, to accomplish this. The ends of the separate wires may not meet exactly, but this is no problem so long as enough collectively meet to form a good solid join. Flux and solder the ends together. File the join with the half-round needle file to remove any sharp edges.

Pickle, rinse and dry the bracelet and round it on the mandrel with the help of the rawhide mallet. Make sure it lies flat on its side by malleting it on the bench anvil. If desired, the bracelet may be given an oval shape to fit the wrist by pressing (by hand) the side with the join toward the opposite side until the oval is achieved. Finish the bracelet by using the same procedures as in the previous projects.

PROJECT 5: Brass/Silver Bangle Bracelet

Two 14-ga. brass wires in 10-in. lengths, and one 40-in. length of 18-ga. silver wire are required for this bracelet. After the wires are annealed, rinsed and dried, the silver wire is bent exactly in half. The free ends are secured in the unshielded jaws of the bench vise while the loop end is placed over a screw hook secured in the chuck of a hand drill as illustrated in Fig. 50. (A large nail inserted in the wire loop can be used in place of the screw hook and hand drill if necessary.) Hold the wire taut with a steady, even pull and twist it rather tightly, but not so much that the wire breaks. When you are done, cut the wire loop in half with the cutting pliers and straighten the severed ends with the form-

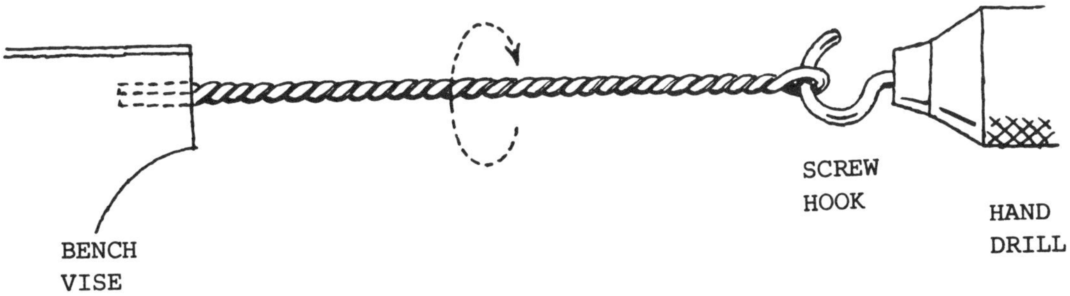

SETUP FOR TWISTING SILVER WIRE

FIGURE 50

ing pliers so that they match the ends that were in the bench vise. Then cut this twisted wire exactly in half, giving you two strands approximately 10 in. in length. Tack their ends together with Medium-grade solder to make them easier to handle. Now place the two strands side by side, and solder the pair of wires together at both ends for a distance of about ¾ of an inch, again using Medium-grade solder. Use binding wire or the crosslock tweezers to hold the wires together. Note that the tweezers, too, must be heated to some degree so that it will not draw the heat away from the join you are trying to make. Be careful not to overload the wires with solder—use just enough to tack them to each other.

Twist the brass wires together with the bench and hand vises, giving them about nine full turns. Apply Medium-grade solder to ¾ in. of each end of the twisted wires in order to tack them together. Flatten about ½ in. of one end of the brass wires with a hammer and do the same with one end of the silver wires. Secure the flattened ends of both sets of wires side by side in the bench vise (see Fig. 51). Hold the brass wires with one hand and with the other

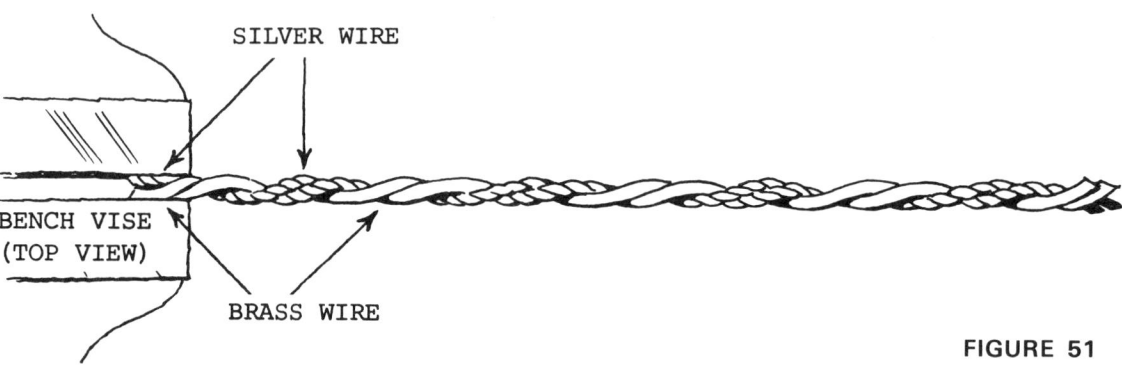

FIGURE 51

hand wrap the silver wires around the brass wires as shown by the arrows. Remove the wires from the vise and cut the ends off evenly. Solder the ends of all the wires together, tieing them with binding wire, if need be, to hold them. Cutting off the damaged ends should leave you with a twisted wire assembly about 8½ in. long. Bend the bracelet to shape, solder the ends together and finish as before. You should be familiar enough with the cleaning, annealing, pickling, smoothing and other processes by now—and the sequence in which to apply each of them—so that it should not be necessary to repeat the instructions each time.

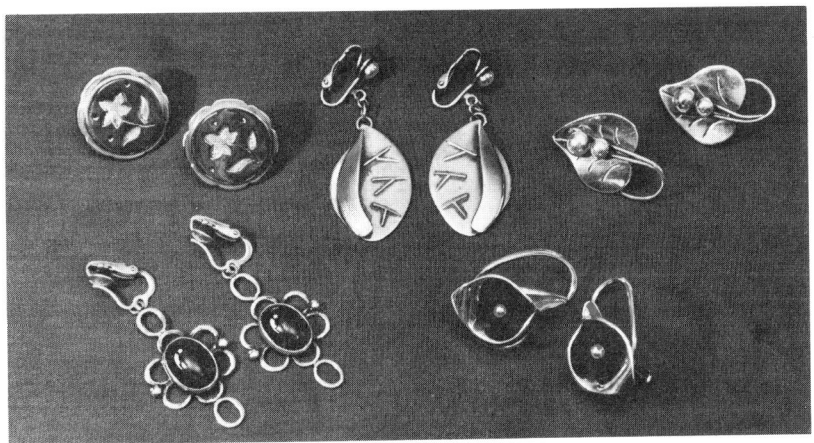

FIGURE 52

5/EARRINGS

There are, basically, two standard types of earrings—the "button" type and the "drop" type. The earrings shown in Fig. 52 do not include any for pierced ears although any of the drop earrings that are shown can be attached to findings made for pierced ears. The buttons for pierced ears are usually very small ornaments inasmuch as large ones have a tendency to swivel down under the earlobe or else lean clumsily away from the earlobe.

PROJECT 6: Brass/Copper Button Earrings

The base plates (A in Fig. 53, two required) are cut from 20-ga. brass. Trace the pattern provided (B in Fig. 53) and transfer it to the brass sheet, using whatever transfer method you prefer. But remember you will be making two identical pieces. Saw out your base plates using a No. 3/0 blade. Use your knife-shaped needle file in finishing the indentations, and your half-round needle file's flat side to finish the rest. Needless to say, the arcs should be uniform in size and curvature on each plate.

Two copper circles, ¾ in. x 20 ga., are also required. Smooth them and transfer each design that is to be drilled and pierced (C and D, Fig. 53). Note that the stems of the flowers curve in opposite directions; this is so that the flowers will both be facing the same way no matter how the lady puts the earrings on. Use a center punch to mark the places for the holes and those where the saw blade is to be threaded in order to pierce out the flower petals and leaves. Drill the holes for the holes with a No. 60 bit and those for the saw blade with a No. 67 bit. Pierce the design, including the flower stem, with a No. 3/0 blade. Remove any burrs and smooth all edges as much as possible. Place the copper disks on the charcoal block, underside up (remember the designs should face in opposite directions), apply flux and arrange snippets of Easy-grade solder spaced ⅛ in. apart around the circumference. Also place a few snippets within the interior portions of the copper circles. Melt the solder and pickle both the brass and copper disks. Place a fluxed brass disk on the charcoal with one pierced piece of copper (fluxed) centered on it, soldered side down as in E, Fig. 53. Heat until the solder flows at all possible points around the perimeter of the copper disk. Repeat with the other pair of disks.

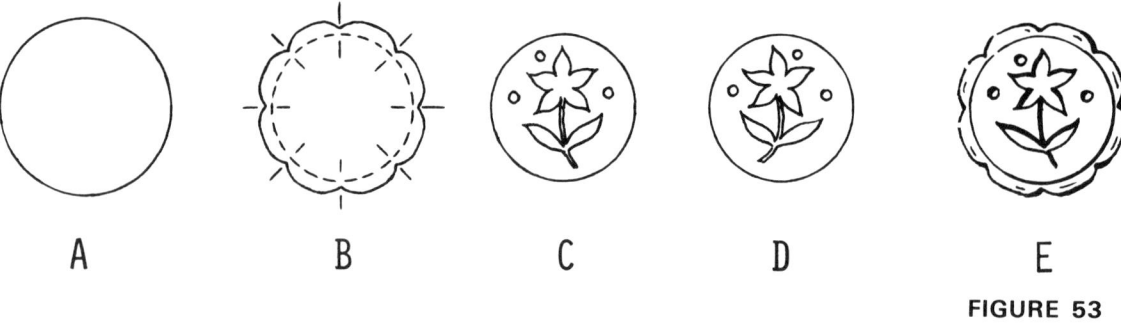

FIGURE 53

Ear-wire findings in brass are attached to this pair of earrings with soft solder. Hold the ear-wires (one at a time) with a crosslock tweezers (see A, Fig. 54), place some soft solder flux in the ear-wires' cups and add a 3/16-in. piece of soft solder. Heat and melt the solder. The cups should be almost full of solder; if not, add more until they are full. Pickle and clean the brass/copper ornaments. Flux them and solder the ear-wires to them, using the soft flame until you see the solder flow (see B, Fig. 54). Pickle, clean up and finish as for the

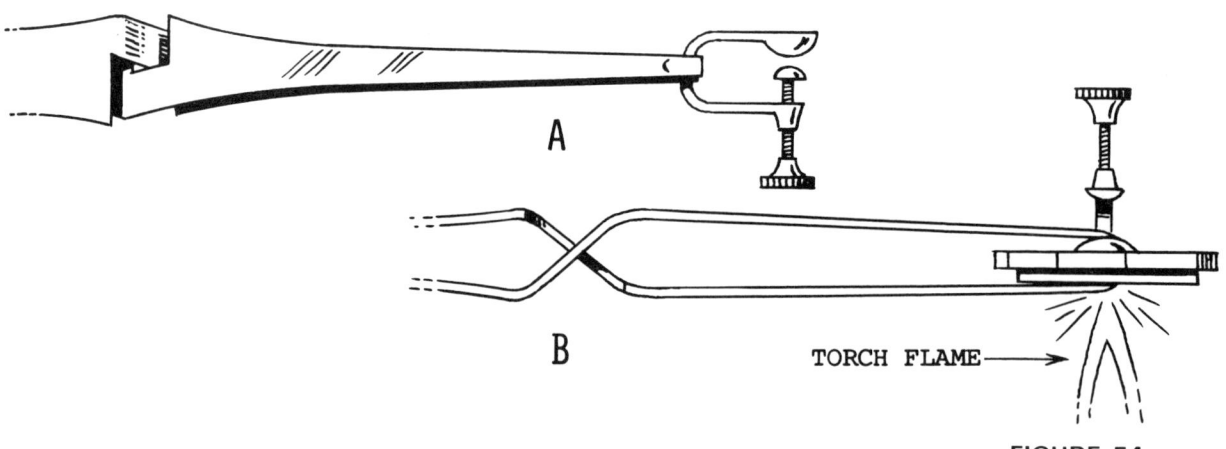

FIGURE 54

EARRINGS

previous projects, but do not use color with this one so that the brass can shine through from behind the copper. To add interest use your scriber to scratch fine lines in every direction inside the flower and leaves (on the brass).

PROJECT 7: Copper/Brass Drop Earrings

In this project note that A in Fig. 55 is cut from 20-ga. copper; B from 20-ga. brass, and that two of each are required. Notice in C and D that these free-form earrings and the applied ornamentation face in opposite directions. The copper pieces are kept flat, but the brass pieces are dapped on the lead block with your largest dapping punch, em-

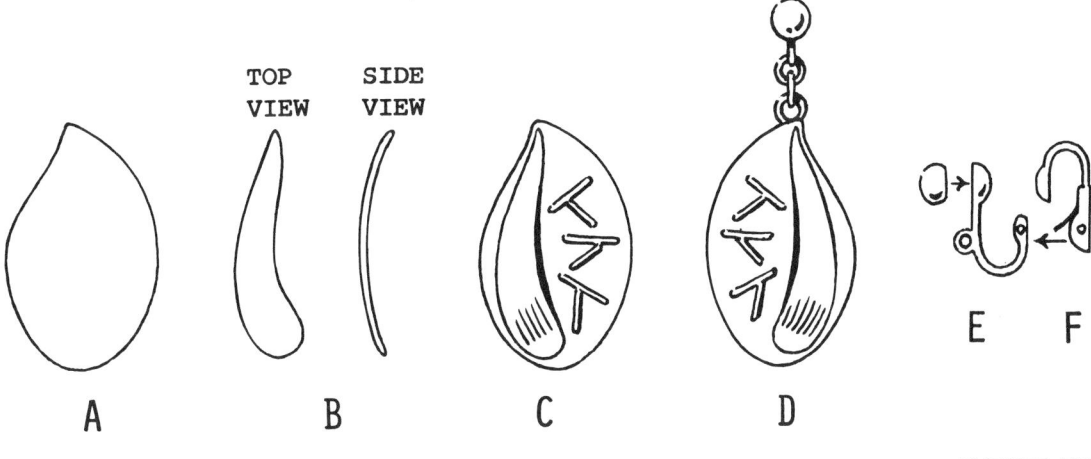

FIGURE 55

bossing hammer or (should you not have either of these) a punch made from a 3/8-in. carriage bolt on which you smooth and polish the head with files and sanding cloths. If the brass pieces curl up or stand away from the copper, flatten them with the mallet so that they stand and fit properly. Be sure to clean the brass pieces with the brass bristle brush to remove any lead particles. Smooth and polish (with tripoli compound only) the copper and brass pieces before soldering them together. To solder the brass ornaments to the copper, first apply Easy-grade solder to the underside of the brass—mainly at the ends where they contact the copper—then solder them onto the copper pieces.

The small T's, also used as applied decoration, are made from 22-ga. brass wire. Each T's crossbar is 3/8 in. long while the vertical bar is 1/4 in. long. Solder the T's together with tiny snippets of Easy-grade solder and then solder them to the copper at the angles shown, again using Easy-grade solder. It will be necessary to protect the brass ornament joins with a small amount of yellow ochre paste. Wash the paste off before the next operation, which should be pickling.

Six copper jump rings, or links, are required (three for each earring) in order to suspend the earrings from the brass earclips used with these earrings. The rings can be bought, but, you can also make them by fastening one end of a piece of annealed 22-ga. copper wire and a 4-penny finishing nail (head off) in the bench vise (see A, Fig. 56) and then winding the wire on the nail for about eight to ten turns. Cut any excess wire off, remove the coil and nail from the vise and the nail from the coil. Secure the coil in the ring clamp (see B, Fig. 56) and saw the links apart with a No. 3/0 blade. The links will fall away as the saw cuts through each one. Hold a link in the pliers and force its ends closed by twisting and pressing with your fingers until the ends fit and match tightly together. Do the same with three more rings. Soft-solder one ring just under the point of each of the copper pieces as shown at D in Fig. 55. Hide the cuts in the rings under the copper. With very little solder, join the seams of the other two rings whose ends you twisted together. Twist an unsoldered ring apart enough to insert in it the ring soldered to one of the copper drops plus one of the soldered rings. Now twist the open ends tightly together and apply a tiny bit of solder (with a small flame) to join the ends. Be careful not to solder the three rings together. Use yellow ochre, if necessary, to protect the previously soldered joins. The rings should look like a short three-link chain as in D, Fig. 55. Complete the other earring to this point.

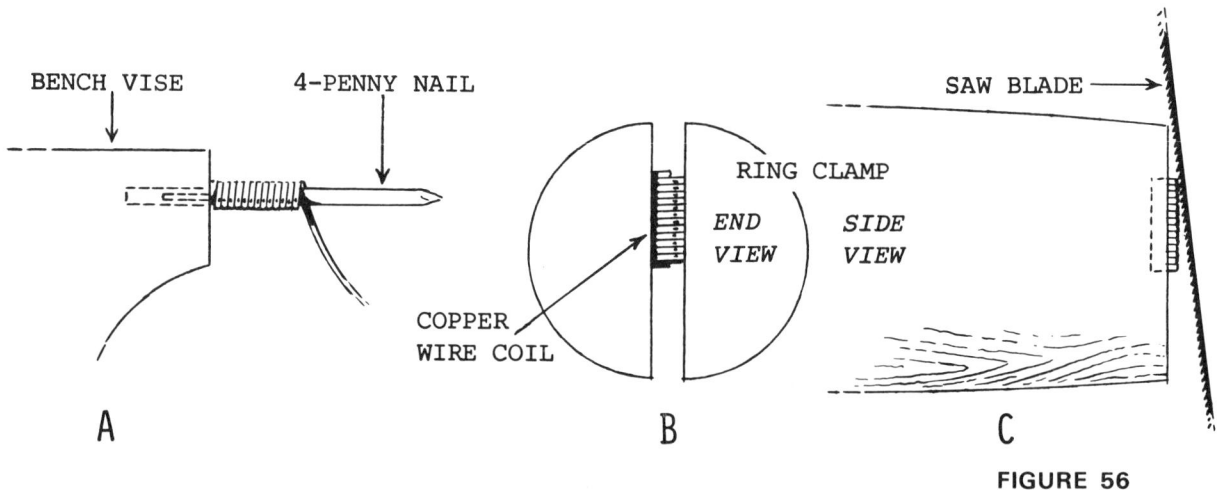

FIGURE 56

Brass earclips are used with these earrings. Remove the part that swivels on a tiny axle (E and F, Fig. 55) by carefully prying it off the axle with your chain-nose pliers. However, first notice how this part and the spring it holds are assembled to the other part so that you will be able to reassemble them again. The purpose in taking them apart is to keep the heat

EARRINGS

from destroying the temper of the spring during the soldering operation. Each bead on the earclips is made from a 1-in. segment of 16-ga. copper wire. They are soft-soldered to the cups (see E, Fig. 55). Reassemble the earclips. Gently twist open the little ring on each earclip and insert the topmost ring of each earring. Then close the ring and touch the join with a tiny bit of soft solder. *Note:* It is in this type of soft-soldering—including the soldering involving the other rings—that a small electric soldering iron comes in handy. Finish the earrings, including coloring them with liver of sulfur.

PROJECT 8: Silver Button Earrings I

The main part of these leaf earrings is cut from 20-ga. silver. The leaf veins (see *A* in Fig. 57) are chased in the manner described in Chapter 3. Note that the earrings face in opposite directions (see *B* and *C*, Fig. 57). The applied stems are made from 18-ga. wire—the longer one is 2 in. long, the shorter is 1⅛ in. long. File one end of the shorter wire so that it blends with the longer one when the two are soldered together with Hard-grade solder as shown in *D*. Curve the joined stems slightly away from each other and solder them to earrings with Medium solder. Curl the free portion of the single stem by grasping its end in your round-nosed pliers and curve the wire around to the back of the earring in the direction in which the illustrations show each should go. Solder the end of the wire to the back of the earring with Medium-grade solder.

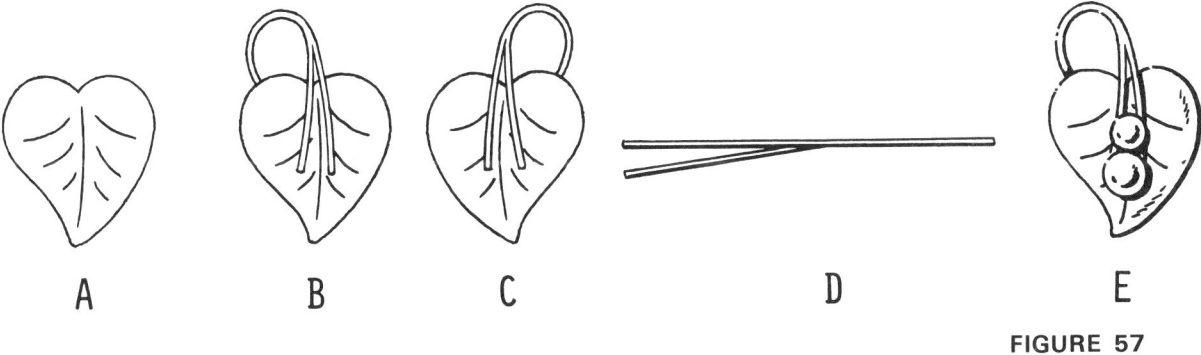

FIGURE 57

The large decorative bead on each earring (see *E*, Fig. 57) has a ¼-in. diameter and is made from scrap silver. The smaller bead (about ⅛-in. diameter) is also made from scrap silver. These are soldered on where shown with Easy-grade solder. The choice of whether to use ear-wires or earclips with these earrings is yours. Regardless of which you choose, soft-solder them on as in the previous projects. Clean up, color and polish the earrings as before.

PROJECT 9: Silver Drop Earrings with Gemstones

These earrings are largely constructed from 18-ga. round wire made into rings of 3/16-in. diameter and joined into the pattern shown at *A*, Fig. 58. The eighteen rings needed can be made by winding the wire on a metal rod, wood dowel or a smoothened 3/16-in. bolt from which the head and threads have been cut off with a hacksaw. The rings are cut apart just as were those in Project 7. Close the rings and hard-solder the ends of each together. The oval-shaped rings that appear at the top and bottom of each earring are made oval by pressing round, soldered rings over the closed ends of the round-nosed pliers. The tiny jump rings at the very top are made from 22-ga. round silver wire wound on a 4-penny finishing nail (such as was also used in Project 7). The darkened circles, shown in *C*, Fig. 58, are silver beads, each one made by melting ¾ in. of 20-ga. silver wire on the charcoal block.

See that all rings lie flat. Assemble the earrings by soldering the rings together (the beads can wait), placing the soldered joins of the rings themselves toward the interior of the earrings where they are less likely to be seen. The outside portions of the round and oval rings —the parts of the perimeters to which the arrows point in *B*, Fig. 58—are flattened slightly with the ball end of the ball peen hammer. This produces tiny facets on the rings which reflect the light in a more interesting way than if they were left fully rounded. Now solder the beads to the earrings where shown in *C*, Fig. 58.

The gemstones used with these earrings are 14 mm. x 10 mm. jade cabochons. Any stones of that basic size can be used. A bezel must be made to hold the stone on the earrings. Here, pure silver bezel wire, 8 ga. x 26 ga., was used. The length required can be determined by cutting a strip of ordinary white adhesive tape ⅛ in. wide and long enough to go one and a half times around the stone (see *D*, Fig. 58). Wrap this around the stone, sticky side in, and put a pencil mark where the tape overlaps its beginning plus 1/32 in. This gives the length of each of the two bezels you will need for the stones, plus a little over for filing the ends square and to allow for the thickness of the wire. Stick the tape to any flat surface and measure off the bezel wire to the required length.

After filing square the ends of the bezel, roughly form each into an oval shape. Bend a piece of your heaviest binding wire into the shape shown in *E*, Fig. 58, and thrust part of the long end into your charcoal block. The dashed-line oval suspended on the wire represents the bezel. This suspension is also shown in *F* which additionally indicates where the Hard-grade solder is to be placed to join the ends of the bezel. Once it is soldered, shape the bezel to fit the stone by pressing it over the stone with your fingers. It should be large enough that the stone can be comfortably placed inside the bezel with the latter resting on a flat surface. If the bezel is too small, it can be enlarged by placing it on a ring mandrel or metal rod and lightly tapping all around its circumference with the flat end of the ball peen hammer. If the bezel is too large, a small piece should be cut out on each side of the join, the ends refiled and the piece resoldered. A bezel that is too large will form ugly wrinkles when you press and form it over the stone.

The stones need base plates on which to rest. Cut two base plates from 20-ga. or 22-ga. silver sheet, each a little larger than the bezel that will be soldered to it. The bezel's bottom

EARRINGS

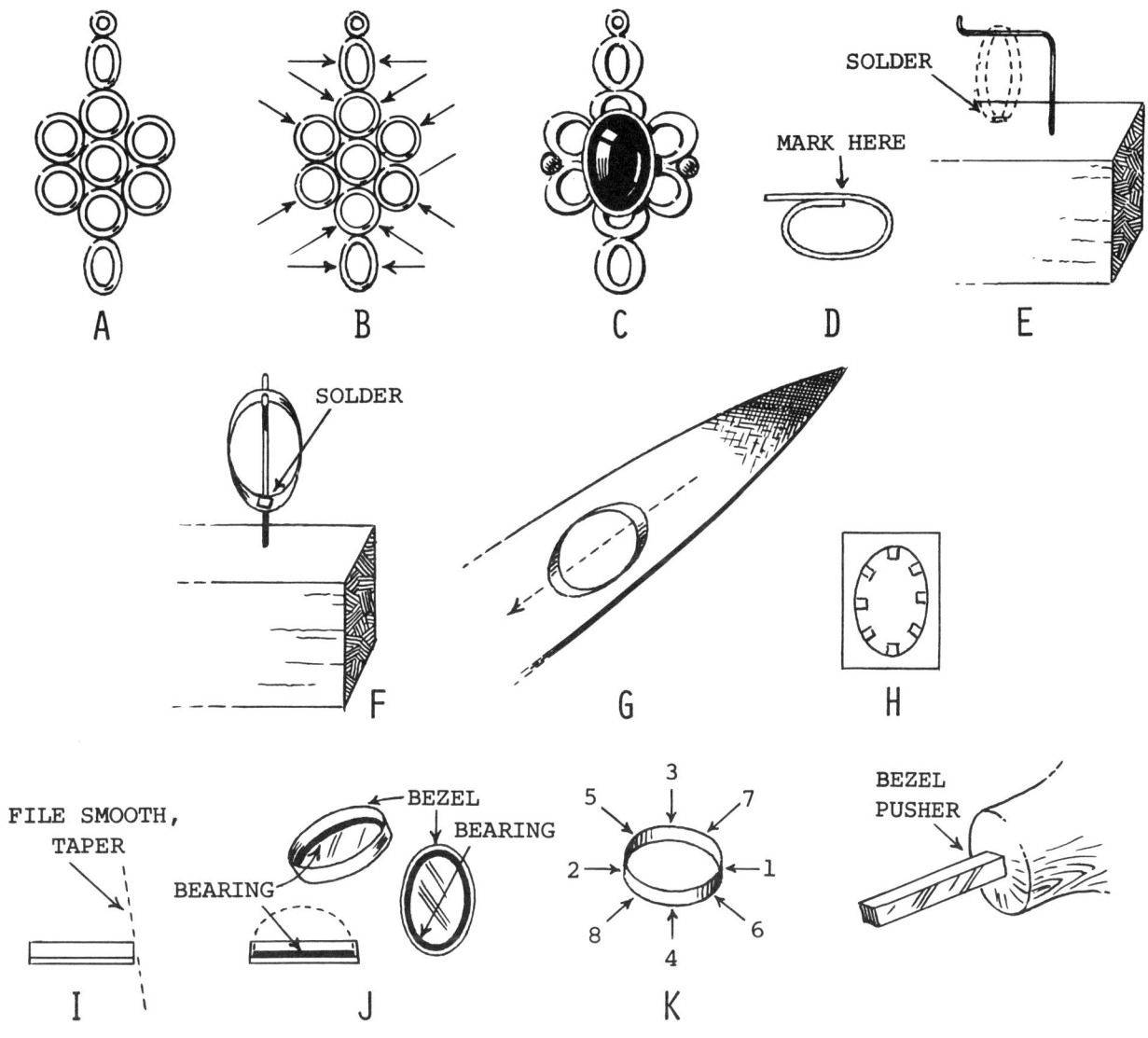

FIGURE 58

edge should touch the bench anvil at every point when placed on this surface. If it does not, tap the top of the bezel lightly with the mallet until it does. Another method for giving the bezel a perfectly flat bottom edge by rubbing it against the teeth of a fine flat file is also shown (see *G*, Fig. 58). Each bezel is handled in the same way. Place one on a fluxed base plate, set Medium-grade solder snippets inside the bezel (see *H*, Fig. 58) and solder the bezel to the plate. Saw the base plates so that their outside contours match those of the bezels. File and smooth the cut edges so that the plates and bezels blend to the degree that the places where they were soldered together are barely visible. File the bezel all around (see *I*, Fig. 58) so that its side tapers from thicker at the bottom to thinner at the top. Smooth the top edge and remove any burrs. Try the stones in the bezels to make sure they still fit and that the bezels have not been distorted as you worked on them. If necessary, use the point of your burnishing tool to reshape the bezel to fit the stone.

Cabochon stones are very frequently set with what is called a "bearing" (see J, Fig. 58). A bearing can be made from a length of 18-ga. round silver wire cut and shaped to fit *inside* the bezel and soldered to the plate and bezel. The purpose of the bearing is to raise the stone higher in the bezel and thus show as much of it as possible while still leaving enough of the bezel to be pressed over the stone to hold it securely. Bearings were used in constructing this pair of earrings, after which the bezel and base-plate assemblies were soldered to the assembled rings as shown in C, Fig. 58. Pickle and clean the full assembly in preparation for mounting the stones.

Place the stones in the bezels, resting them on the bearings. With the aid of a stone pusher, begin pressing in the bezel against the stone in the sequence indicated by the numbers in K, Fig. 58. A stone pusher can be bought, but it is basically a 3-in. length of steel rod, 3/16 in. square, inserted into a handle made from a ⅝-in. or ¾-in. wood dowel. The pusher's working end is slightly rounded to avoid having it cut into the sides of the bezel. After the bezel is pushed in at the initial eight points (do not use much pressure at first) begin to press the bezel in at alternate points between the initial eight. Then switch to the curved burnisher and, with a steady pressure and sliding motion, burnish the bezel until it lies smoothly around the stone at every point. Any tool marks left on the bezel may be removed by careful use of the small files, small pieces of sanding cloth and the Scotch stone. Keep these away from the gemstone, so as not to mar its high polish.

These earrings are given the usual finishing treatment—including coloring—and are attached to ear-wires or earclips according to the wearer's preference. By using earring findings that come with a half dome or bead ornament already attached (as was done here) we obviate the need to make and solder beads onto the findings.

PROJECT 10: Silver Button Earrings II

The main body of these earrings is fashioned from heart-shaped pieces of 20-ga. silver. Two pieces cut to the shape shown in A, Fig. 59 are required. It is best to anneal these pieces and to smooth and polish them to some degree before proceeding to the next stage. Notice in B and C that the lobes of the heart are bent around and over each other with the round-nosed pliers. In B, the left lobe is curved around first, with the right lobe brought around to overlap the left. In C, the opposite procedure is followed. In short, the earrings should face opposite directions. When looking down into the earring, it should be as if you were looking into a tulip or daffodil. The overlapping lobes must be soldered together (it may be necessary to tap them with your mallet to bring them in close contact with each other). Use Hard-grade solder. There will be a hole where the two lobes meet at the very bottom, but the "jack-in-the-pulpit" ornamentation fits in this. Curve the

EARRINGS

point of the heart backward with the round-nosed pliers (see *D*, Fig. 59). Pickle the earrings.

The "jack-in-the-pulpit" ornamentation starts out as a 3½-in. length of annealed 14-ga. wire (two are required). Each wire should be as straight and clean as possible. A bead is made on one end of each wire by holding the wire in a crosslock tweezers, end pointing down to the charcoal block (see *E*, Fig. 59). The end of the wire is held about ¼ in. above the block and the torch flame is directed at this end. In time, the first ¼ in. or so of the wire will turn white hot, melt and begin to flow upon itself, forming a bead. Have the flame follow this upflow for a second or two, then remove it. A fair-sized bead can be produced on the wire, but it must be watched closely so that it does not become so hot and large that it melts itself off the wire. Cool and pickle the wire.

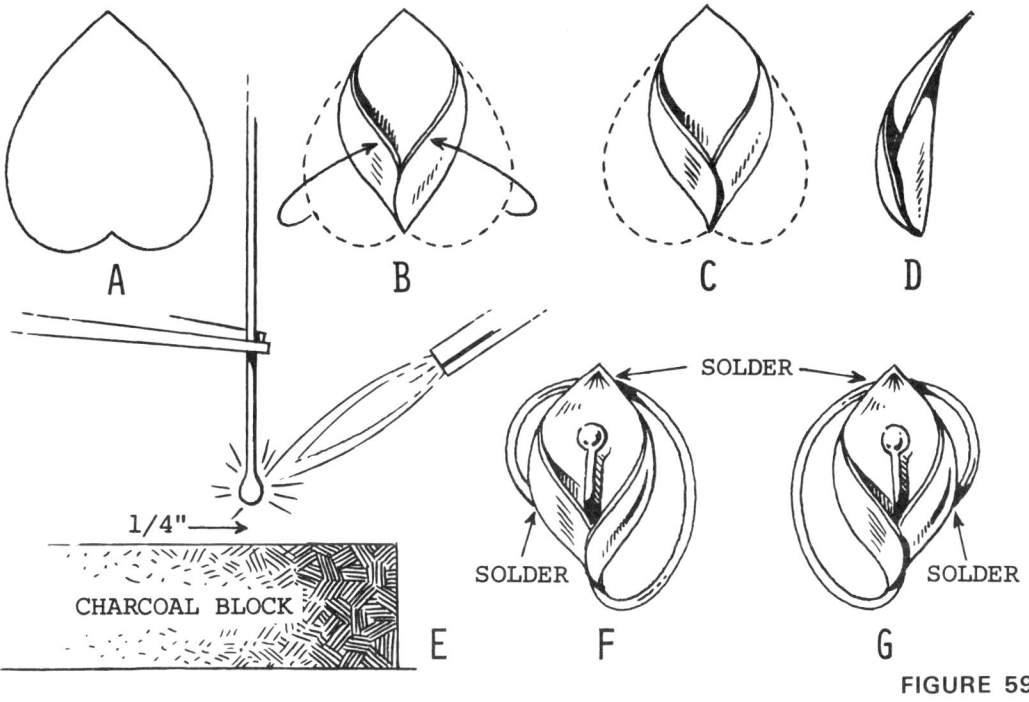

FIGURE 59

F and *G*, Fig. 59, show how the wires are inserted through the holes in the bottom of each earring. The wires should be soldered in place there (Medium-grade solder) before they are bent around the earrings. The bending is done with the round-nosed pliers. The wire is soldered with Medium-grade solder where it curves under what was initially the point of the heart shape. Use the crosslock tweezers, if necessary, to hold it in place. It is also soldered with Easy-grade solder where its free end comes around to meet the side of the earring. If the wire is too long to make a graceful, proportionate bend, cut it to an appropriate length and file the end so that it butts against the side of the earring closely. Either earwires or earclips may be used. Finish as before.

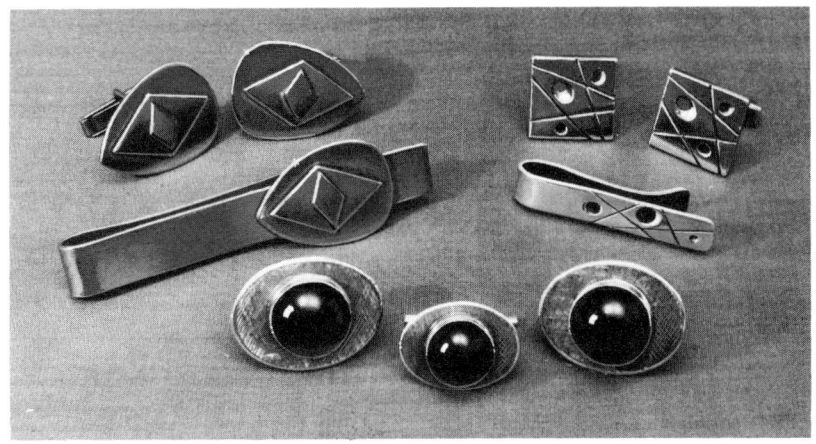

FIGURE 60

6/CUFF LINKS WITH MATCHING TIE ORNAMENTS

There was a time when men wore as many gems and jewelry ornaments as women. This, like so many other things, changed in past years to the point where men wore very little jewelry, but it may now be changing again. At any rate, cuff links and tie ornaments are still a part of most men's wardrobe. Here are a few examples of items you can make to enhance any man's over-all appearance. (See Fig. 60.)

PROJECT 11: Copper/Brass Cuff Links and Tie Bar

The basic task in constructing this cuff-link and tie-bar set is cutting out the required number of pieces of each form and soldering them together in the pattern as shown in the illustration (see Fig. 61). *A* is a free-form shape cut from 18-ga. copper, *B* is a diamond (½ in. to a side) cut from 18-ga. brass, and *C* is a smaller diamond (¼ in. to a side) cut from 18-ga. copper. Three of each shape are required for the set. In this project, the method of assembling the brass diamond to the copper free form and the copper diamond to the brass is called "sweat soldering." To do this, you inscribe the outline of the brass diamond on the copper free form with your scriber, apply flux to the copper inside this outline, place snippets of Medium-grade solder within the outline (see *D*, Fig. 61) and then set the brass diamond on the solder pieces, making sure that it is properly aligned with its outline. Apply heat and watch for the brass to settle down and a bright line of molten solder to appear around its perimeter. Have your soldering pusher ready in case the brass moves out of place.

The same steps are followed in sweat soldering the copper diamond in place (see E, Fig. 61). Use Easy-grade solder this time.

Brass cuff-link backs were used with this jewelry. The cups are filled with soft solder and the backs are soldered to the decorative parts. Make certain that they are oriented as shown in F, Fig. 61.

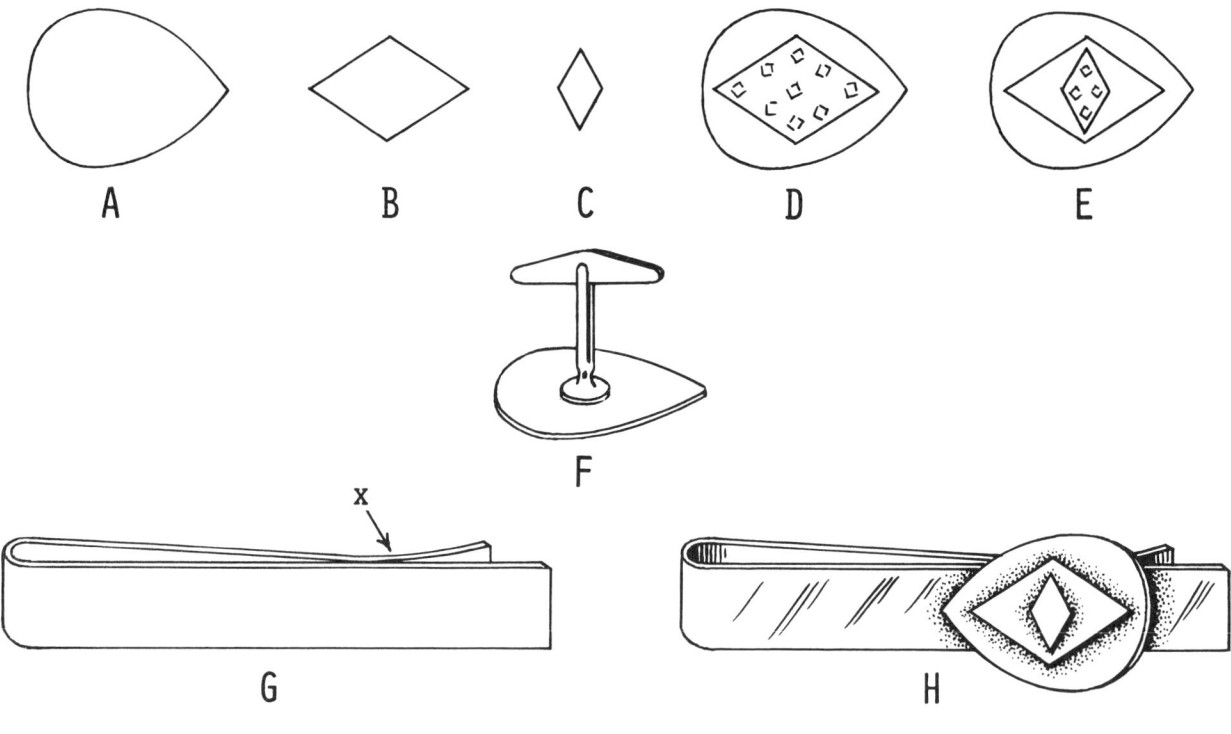

FIGURE 61

The main part of the tie bar is a piece of sheet copper 5½ in. long by 7/16 in. wide by 16 ga. After smoothing all edges and removing any blemishes from the flat surfaces, bend back the section labeled X (in G, Fig. 61) with your round-nosed pliers. Use a pencil to mark off a distance of 3 in. from the other end of the tie bar. Place a headless 16-penny nail upright in your bench vise and bend the tie bar around it until the curved part X meets the tie bar proper. Set the bar on the bench anvil and strike this last bend with the mallet to add some spring to the metal at this point. Do not close the gap too much because space is needed for the tie and shirt-front which the tie bar grips when it is in place. Soft-solder the third ornament to the bar as shown in H, Fig. 61. The set looks better if antiqued with liver of sulfur than if left plain. The tie ornament can be soft-soldered to an alligator-type tie clip should you prefer this to the bar.

CUFF LINKS WITH MATCHING TIE ORNAMENTS

PROJECT 12: Silver Cuff Links and Tie Bar

This abstract set of cuff links is made from ¾ in. x ¾ in. x 16-ga. silver. The surface lines shown in *A* and *B*, Fig. 62, are cut in with the knife-shaped needle file to a depth of at least 1/32 in. The holes are drilled through with the following bits: the largest is drilled with the No. 30, those in the upper left with the No. 53, and the others on the right side with the No. 45. Note that one hole (on the right in *B*) is drilled in a different place from its counterpart in *A*. This is a matter of personal choice. The shaded portions on each hole indicate that the round needle file is used at an angle to file the upper and lower surfaces so that the holes become oval or oblong rather than remain round.

Use cuff-link backs that come in three parts for this set. They should be hard-soldered to the backs of the decorative sections with Easy-grade solder.

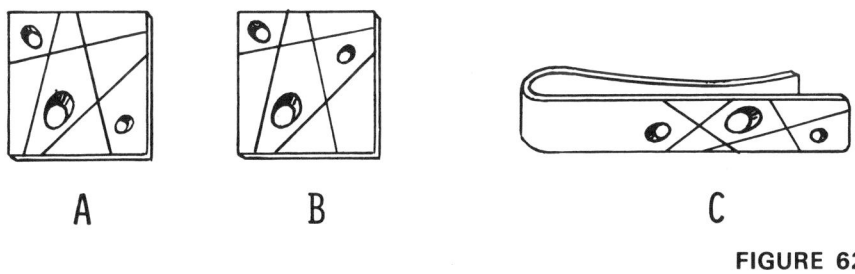

FIGURE 62

The tie bar is made from 18-ga. silver, 3¼ in. long by ¼ in. wide (see *C*, Fig. 62). The lines are filed into it and the holes are all drilled and filed oval as on the cuff links. Although smaller than the tie bar in the previous project, it is bent to shape in the same way except that 1¾ in. is marked off as the front of the bar. The lines and holes in the set will stand out more interestingly if the set is antiqued in the usual way.

PROJECT 13: Silver Cuff Links and Tie Tack with Gemstones

The stones in this cuff-link and tie-tack set are round, black onyx cabochons. Those in the cuff links are each 24 mm. in diameter while the one in the tie tack is 12 mm. in diameter. Any round cabochon of the same dimensions can, of course, be used. See *A*, Fig. 63, for the shape and size of the cuff-link plates. The plate for the tie tack is smaller, of course. All are cut from 18-ga. silver sheet. The top surfaces are given a pseudo-Florentine finish (see *B*, Fig. 63) by cross-hatching lines in three different directions on these surfaces with the scriber and rule. The lines drawn in each direction are about 1/32 in. apart. Craftsmen usually use special engraving tools, called "graver liners," for this finish, but a reasonably close facsimile of the real thing can be achieved by the method suggested here. Round the

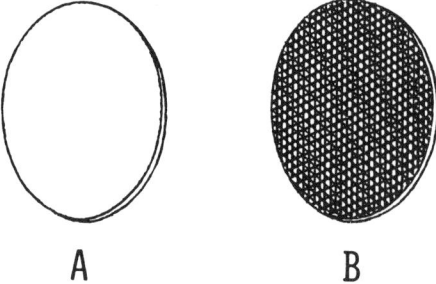

FIGURE 63

edges of all the plates with files and sanding cloth to produce plain, shiny edges that will frame the Florentine texture and thus emphasize and enhance it.

Measure and make the bezels for the stones from 8-ga. x 26-ga. bezel wire as you did in an earlier project. See that they fit the stones comfortably. Because the cuff link and tie tack plates themselves will back up the stones, the bezels can be soldered directly to the plates with Medium-grade solder, placing them as seems pleasing to your eye. Bearings were used under all the stones, however, in order to make the cabochons appear as high as possible. Bearings of 18-ga. wire still leave enough height to the bezels to hold the stones. Use Easy-grade solder to fix the cuff-link backs to the cuff links and soft solder to attach the part of the tie tack to the ornament. Set the stones after all the soldering is done, employing the stone pusher and burnisher.

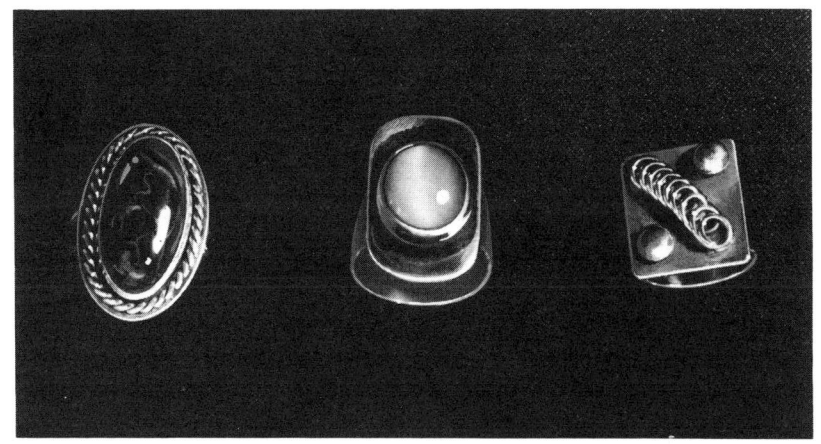

FIGURE 64

7/RINGS

There are many ways in which rings can be made. Three of the most often used methods are demonstrated here (see Fig. 64). A person's finger or ring size is best measured with the ring sizer. However, since translating the numbers on the sizer's ring into the required length of the ring shank is difficult, the following chart of common finger sizes is offered with the understanding that 1/32 in. to 1/16 in. more must be added to the shank's length to take care of the metal's thickness.

Finger Size	Shank (Inches)	Finger Size	Shank (Inches)	Finger Size	Shank (Inches)	Finger Size	Shank (Inches)
6	2-1/16	8	2-3/8	9½	2-15/32	11	2-11/16
6½	2-3/32	8½	2-7/16	10	2-9/16	11½	2-3/4
7	2-1/8	9	2-1/2	10½	2-5/8	12	2-13/16
7½	2-1/4						

PROJECT 14: Lady's Brass/Copper Ring

The shank for this ring was made for a Size 7 finger. A simple way to obtain a pattern for the ring's shank is to fold a small piece of paper in four parts (see *A*,

99

Fig. 65), draw one-fourth of the shank on the paper and then cut out the design with the paper still folded. When the cutout is opened, it will appear as in *B*—the dashed lines indicate where the paper was folded. The paper is glued to a sheet of 16-ga. brass and the shank is cut out with a No. 2/0 blade. The next step is to mallet the shank on your ring mandrel (around the No. 7 graduation or whatever the size of your shank is) so as to bring the ends together as in *C*. The ends are soldered together with the solder (Medium-grade) placed as in *D*. *Note:* Use sufficient solder so that the join is completely filled.

The plate for the ornamental part of the ring is 16-ga. copper, measuring ¾ in. by ⅝ in. The wire coil soldered to it is made from 20-ga. brass wire wound on a ⅛ in. diameter nail or other suitable mandrel. (See *E* in Fig. 65.) About nine to ten turns of the wire are required. Before soldering it to the copper plate, the coil should be pressed out flat with your fingers and then tapped with the mallet to flatten it further. Two brass beads are required, each fused from 1 in. x 18-ga. wire. The coil and beads are soldered on with Medium-grade solder. (See *F* in Fig. 65.)

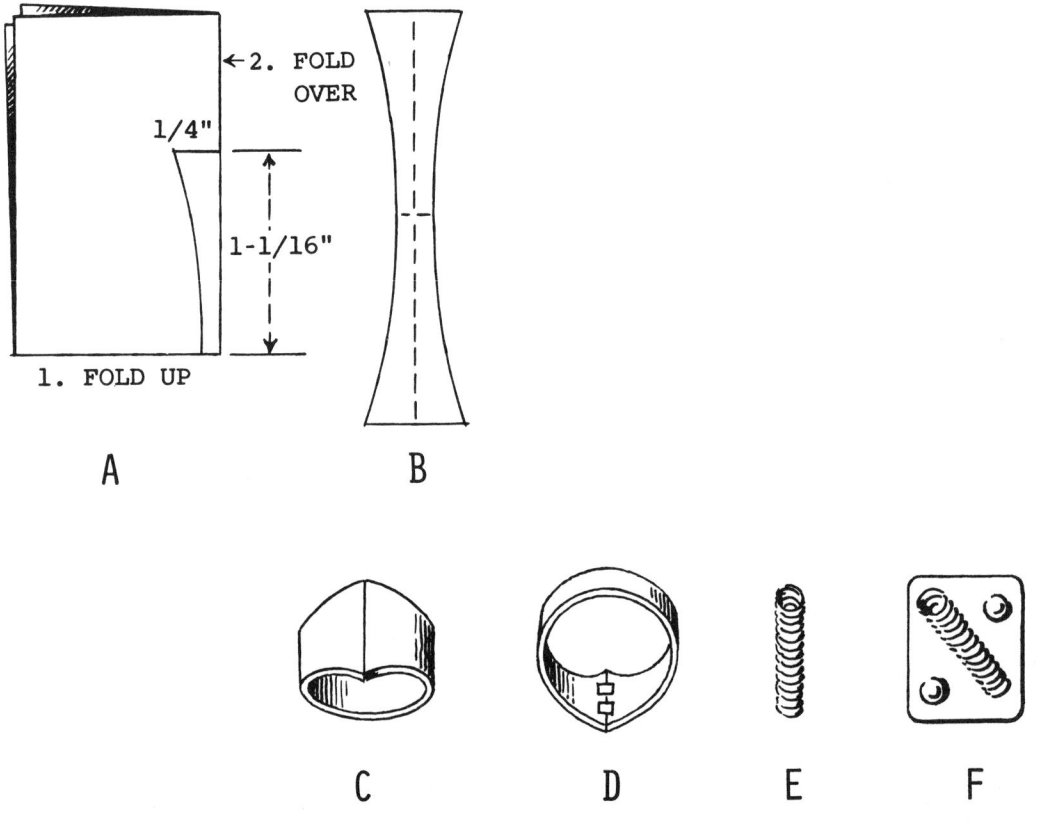

FIGURE 65

RINGS

Prior to soldering the shank to the ornament, file a flat on the shank about 3/32 in. wide down the length of the join in order to provide more area for the solder. Use binding wire to tie the shank to the ornament, placing the shank's join against the copper. Place snippets of Easy-grade solder all around the sections where the shank and copper are in contact with each other. If any filing is needed inside the shank, use the half round side of your ring file for this. The inside of the shank can be polished by tieing a piece of thin felt or cotton flannel around a dowel of suitable diameter. Color and finish the ring as you would any other piece.

PROJECT 15: Man's Silver Ring

The over-all design for this ring can be produced on folded paper (see A, Fig. 66) as in the preceding project. B shows how the design looks when the paper is unfolded. This particular ring was made to fit an 8½ finger size, but it can be made to fit any size of finger simply by referring to the chart given at the start of this chapter. The shank of the ring—which includes a section on which the ornamental part is mounted—is cut from 18-ga. silver. The shank is first curved at the 8½ graduation on the ring mandrel, and then the ends are curved to meet as shown in C. Solder the ends together with Medium-grade solder. Use this section as the pattern from which to enscribe a top plate for the ring on 18-ga. or 20-ga. silver (see D, Fig. 66). Cut this plate about 1/16 in. larger all around than the enscribed line so as to provide a little shelf for the solder snippets when the plate is soldered to the rest of the ring. This excess shelf is then filed off.

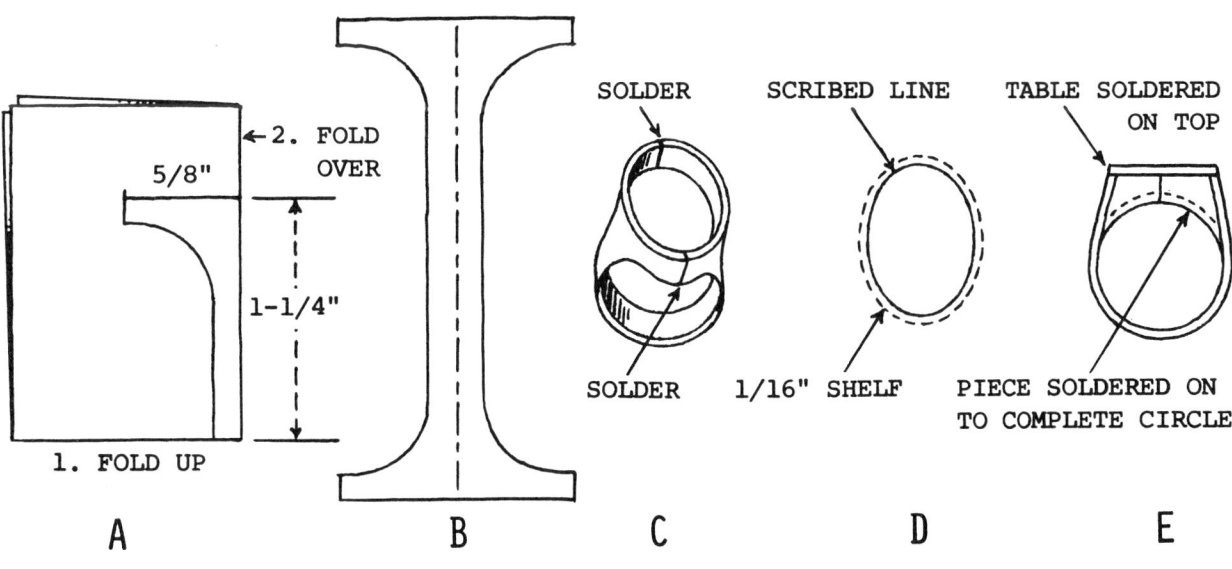

FIGURE 66

A piece of 18-ga. silver should be cut to fit so as to complete the circle of the shank (see E, Fig. 66). Once this piece is shaped, solder it in place with Medium-grade solder. Either a bezel for a stone (as with the ring illustrated in Fig. 64), a person's initial or initials, a fraternal emblem or other decorative effect suitable for a male can be soldered to the top plate for decoration. Most libraries have books which show different styles of alphabets. In these you may select letter styles that will appeal to the ultimate wearer's taste or to your own taste, as you prefer.

PROJECT 16: Lady's Silver Ring with Gemstone

The oval stone called chrysocolla (chrys'-o-col'-la) set on this ring measures 23 mm. x 13 mm., which is not a standard size. You may use any standard or nonstandard size of oval stone by cutting the bezel and plate to fit the stone. In measuring the plate, made from 20-ga. silver sheet, allow for the twisted 20-ga. wire used as a frame around the bezel plus a little bit more. The length of each of the two wires to be twisted should be about 1 in. longer than the perimeter of the bezel. A and B in Fig. 67 are provided primarily to show how the ornamental parts of the ring are combined. A bearing may be used under the stone, if desired.

The technique (not previously discussed) that this project introduces is the method employed to make a ring shank out of wire. The method shown here is but one example. Two pieces of 12-ga. round wire are cut to the finger size (as shown on the chart above), plus 1/16 in. more for the wire's thickness. They are bent to the shape shown in C and hard-soldered together for a distance of about ½ in. to ⅝ in. along their midpoints. File the ends of the wire

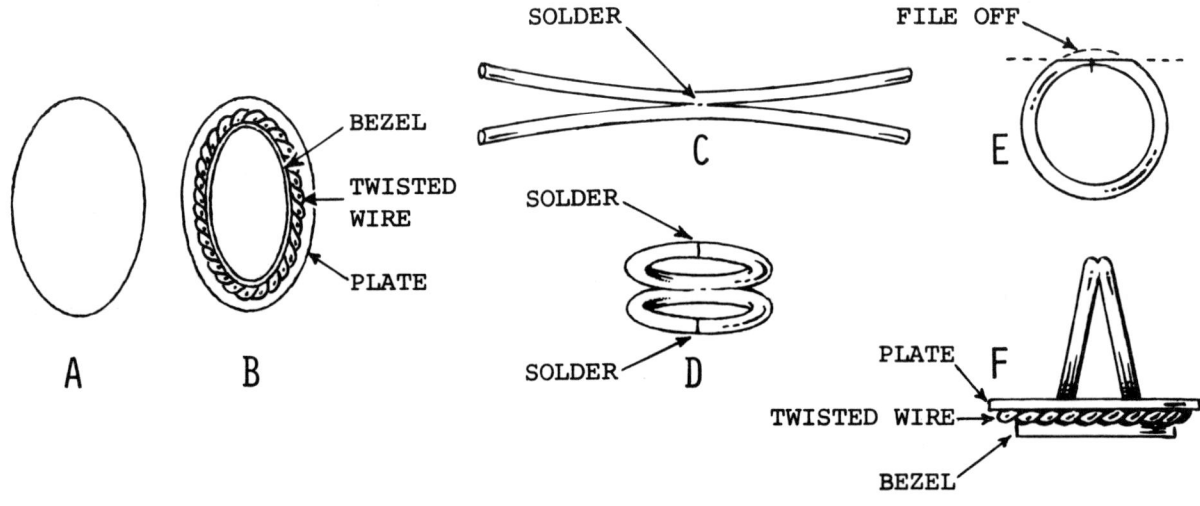

FIGURE 67

flat and use your round-nosed pliers to bring the ends together as in *D*. Solder the ends together with Easy-grade solder. Place the soldered rings on the ring mandrel and use your mallet to make them perfectly round. Turn the rings over on the mandrel so that both are exactly the same shape and size.

File a flat area on both rings at the joins as indicated in *E*. The purpose is to provide a larger area for the solder in the next soldering step which is shown in *F*. Easy-grade solder may be used. Do as much filing and smoothing as possible before setting the stone to avoid damaging the stone's polish.

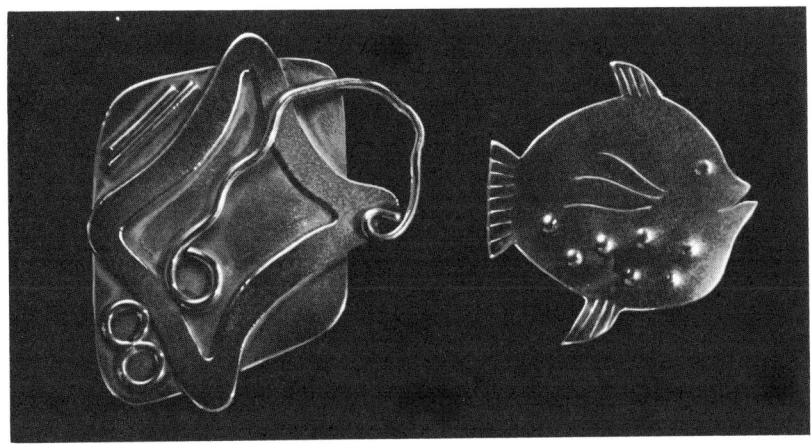

FIGURE 68

8/PINS AND BROOCHES

If you have faithfully followed the projects as successively presented so far, you have acquired most of the skills needed to create a pin or brooch, such as those shown in Fig. 68. The process that will be new in this project involves the application of the joint, safety catch and pin stem. Herewith, then, are two projects designed to acquaint you with the technique. Incidentally, in jewelry the term pin and brooch are used interchangeably. Pin is used here because it is simpler.

PROJECT 17: Copper/Brass Pin

Fig. 69 shows the parts that constitute the free-form pin and how these parts are applied. *A* is the pin's backing cut from 18-ga. copper; *B* is cut from 18-ga. brass, with the section marked with the *X*'s pierced out. In *C*, the two straight wires in the upper left are 16-ga. brass, one ¾ in. long, the other ⅝ in. long. The long wire that is curved and bent with the round-nosed pliers is also 16-ga. brass. Start with a piece 5 in. long and cut off the excess, if necessary. The two brass rings in the lower left are 18-ga. by 3/16 in. diameter. All these parts may be applied to the copper with Medium-grade solder.

D, in Fig. 69, shows the reverse side of the pin and the position of the safety catch and joint. There are four basic principles that apply to the proper positioning of these items as well as the pin stem:

1. The joint and catch must be positioned above the center of the pin, otherwise the top of the pin will lean forward when it is worn.

2. With the back of the pin facing you, the joint is always positioned on the right side (this is still a "right-handed" world).

105

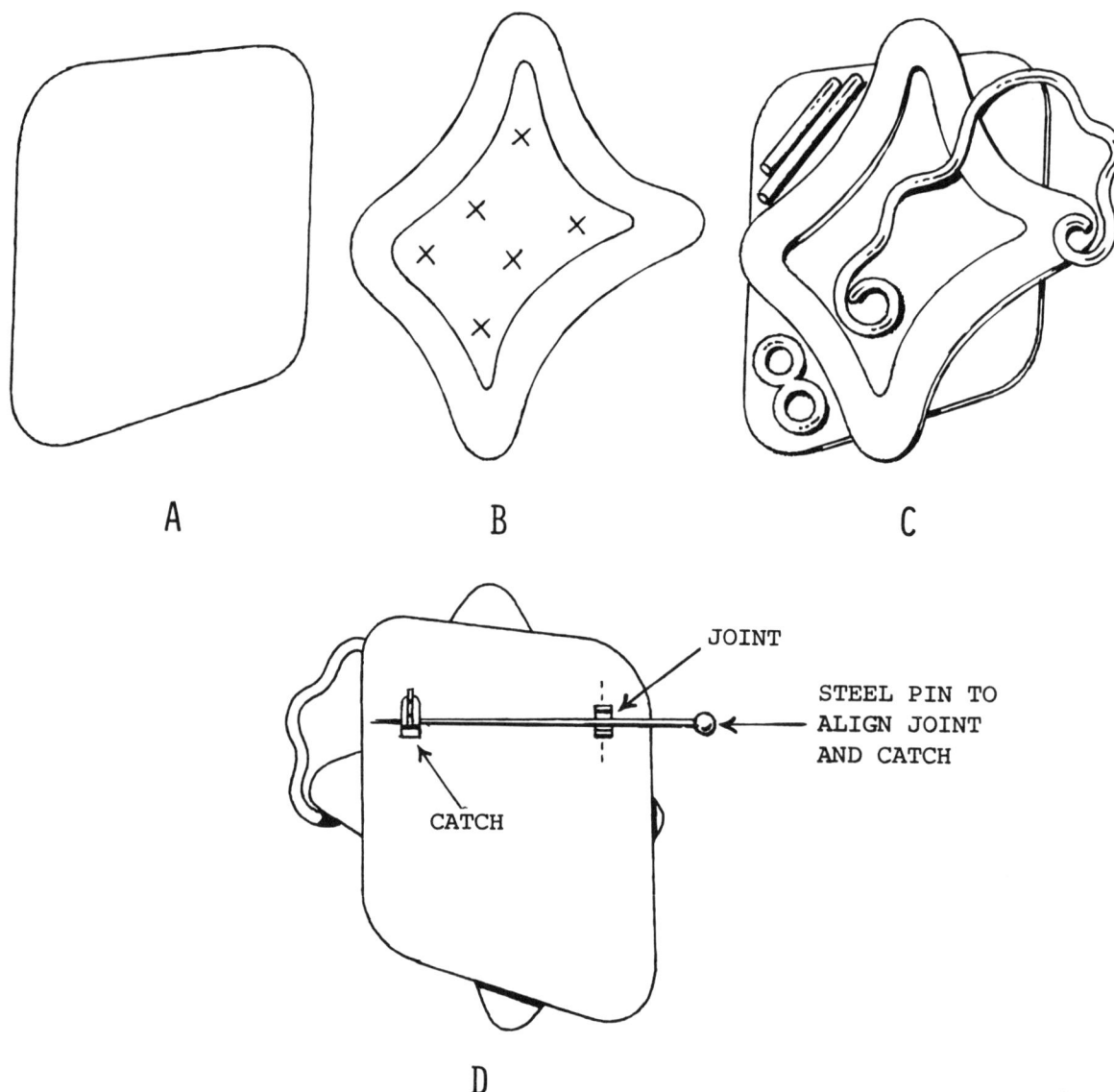

FIGURE 69

3. The opening of the catch faces downward to give added security in the event the catch is opened accidentally.

4. The pin stem is never emplaced until *all* soldering operations have been completed.

The joint is soldered in position first using Easy-grade solder. This is best done by marking the place for the joint, fluxing it, and placing one or two snippets of solder on the spot. Melt the solder. Dip the metal in water to cool it and then dry it. Flux the solder, file or sand the

PINS AND BROOCHES

bottom of the joint so that it is clean and then place it in the correct position on the solder. Remelt the solder so as to affix the joint. Remember to heat the mass of metal rather than concentrating the flame on the joint itself. You may wish to use the crosslock tweezers to hold the joint in the proper position.

A simple implement is recommended as an aid in determining the placement and the soldering in place of the safety catch. The implement is a thin steel pin about 2½ in. long. An embroidery needle, a short hat pin or the type of pin used to fasten a corsage of flowers—any or each of these is suitable. The hat or corsage pin usually has a pearl-like bead or other decoration on one end which should be broken off with a hammer or pliers. In use, the catch is closed and the point of the pin is fixed in the small opening of the catch. The steel pin with the catch (standing upright) is set in the joint. It is moved until the catch is where it should be (see *D*, Fig. 69). Mark the place with the scriber and remove the catch and pin. Place one or two snippets of Easy-grade solder on the fluxed spot and melt the solder. Cool and dry the jewelry. Reflux the spot, file or sand the bottom of the catch so that it is bright-clean and reposition it and the steel pin as before, with the bottom of the catch resting on the solder. Reheat the full mass of the jewelry until the solder flows. Remove the steel pin. Clean up and do most of the polishing of the brooch before fixing the pin stem in the joint.

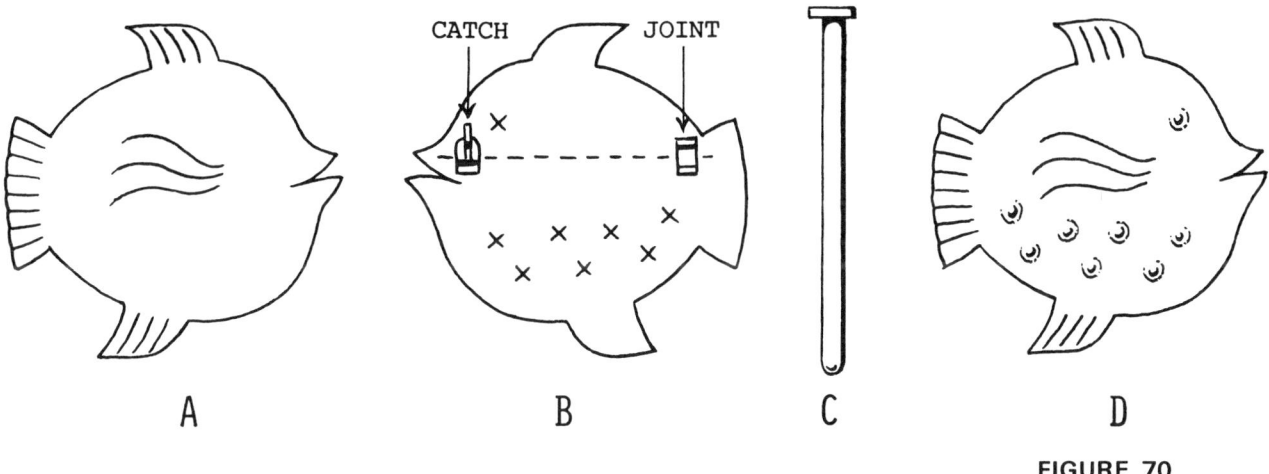

FIGURE 70

As was indicated in Chapter 1 in the Findings section, some pin stems come with the rivets already set in them. If this is the type you have, it is a simple matter to set the rivet ends in the holes of the matching joint, squeeze the joint together with the flat-nosed pliers and then spread the rivet ends by hammering them on the bench anvil as you did in the silver cuff-link projects. If the pin stem has no pre-set rivet you will need nickel silver rivet wire. This is sold by jewelry supply houses in packets of assorted diameters. Select one that snugly fits the holes in the pin stem and joint. Cut off a length that permits the rivet to extend about 1/32 in. from each side of the joint. Broaden the rivet ends as before.

It is often necessary to cut a pin stem shorter so that its pointed end will not extend beyond the back of the pin and thus be seen from the front. This can easily be done with the cutting pliers or the jeweler's saw, after which a new point should be filed on the pin stem. Sand the marks of the file away.

PROJECT 18: Silver Pin

This project is provided mainly to give you additional experience in chasing, dapping and the placement of the joint, safety catch and pin stem. After the pin is cut out, chase the fins, tail, body of the fish and the curve of its mouth as shown in *A*, Fig. 70. *B* shows the reverse side of the fish and the *X*'s represent the points at which the eye and—for want of a better word—the warts on the lower part of the fish's body are bumped up so that they stand out on the front side. The bumping is done on the lead block and the implement used can be improvised from a 20-penny nail (or a piece of steel of similar length and diameter) on which the sharp point is filed down to a rather broad curve or dome shape (see *C*, Fig. 70). Now refer again to *B* in Fig. 70 which indicates where the joint and catch, respectively, should be placed. Drawing *D* shows the appearance of the pin when it is completed.

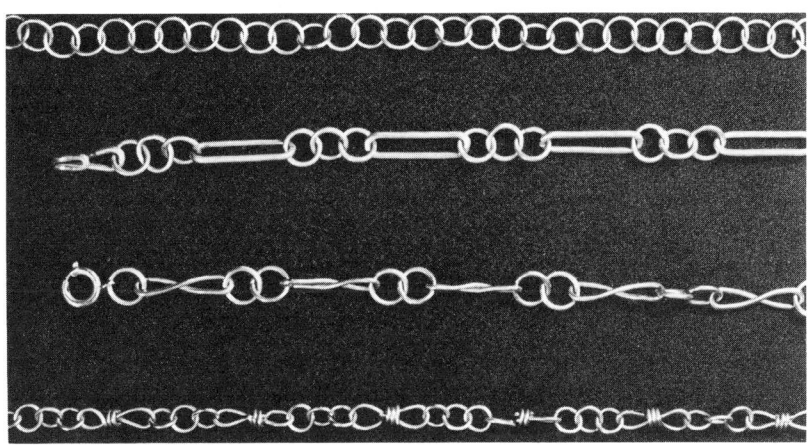

9/CHAIN MAKING

FIGURE 71

Commercially made chains can, of course, be bought, but chains can also be made by the craftsman in literally dozens of different styles, depending, fundamentally, on the size and shape of the rods, mandrels or specially made jigs used to form the links. It is difficult to say just how long a chain should be. This will depend, first, on the ornament to be suspended from it and, second and equally important, on the size and physical make-up of the person who will wear the chain and the ornament. You will have to use your own judgment in this. Three styles of chain are explored here in order to give you some experience in chain making. (See Fig. 71.)

PROJECT 19: Round Link Chain

You have already constructed jump rings which, if enough are linked together, will produce a simple chain. For this project you may use any metal you desire. Remember to anneal the wire. The links for a round link chain are formed by wrapping wire of the desired thickness around a rod or mandrel of the desired inside diameter and then cutting across the formed coiled wire with a jeweler's saw to get single links. One half of the links are closed in the same way as the jump rings and soldered individually. In soldering (using Easy-grade solder) as many of the closed links as possible are set on the charcoal block with the seam to be soldered facing away from you (see A, Fig. 72). Some craftsmen prefer to apply the solder with the pusher (see the Soldering section in Chapter 3).

When half the links are soldered, two soldered links are joined by an unsoldered link to form a group of three links. After closing the unsoldered link, it may be positioned for soldering on the asbestos pad or charcoal block as seen in B, Fig. 72. Groups of three are joined to form a chain of the desired length.

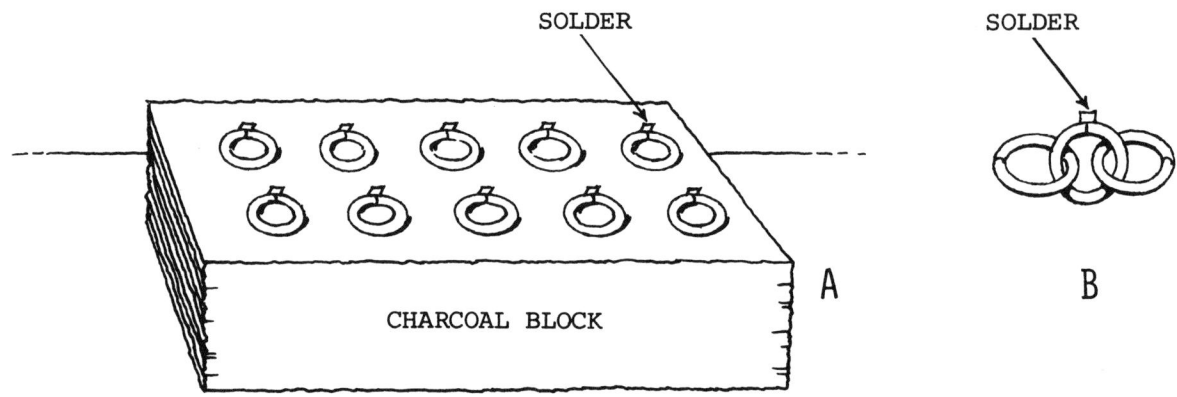

FIGURE 72

PROJECT 20: Handmade Chain

This chain is for the pendant which we are going to make in Project 22. It consists of elliptical links connected by three round links (see *A*, Fig. 73). The round links are made from 18-ga. brass and are shaped on a ¼-in. diameter rod. The elliptical links (of 16-ga. brass) are shaped around a jig made by hammering two 10-penny finishing nails, ¾ in. apart, into a block of wood as shown in *B*. The nail heads are cut off with the jeweler's saw after they are in the wood. The wood block is secured in the bench vise and the wire is

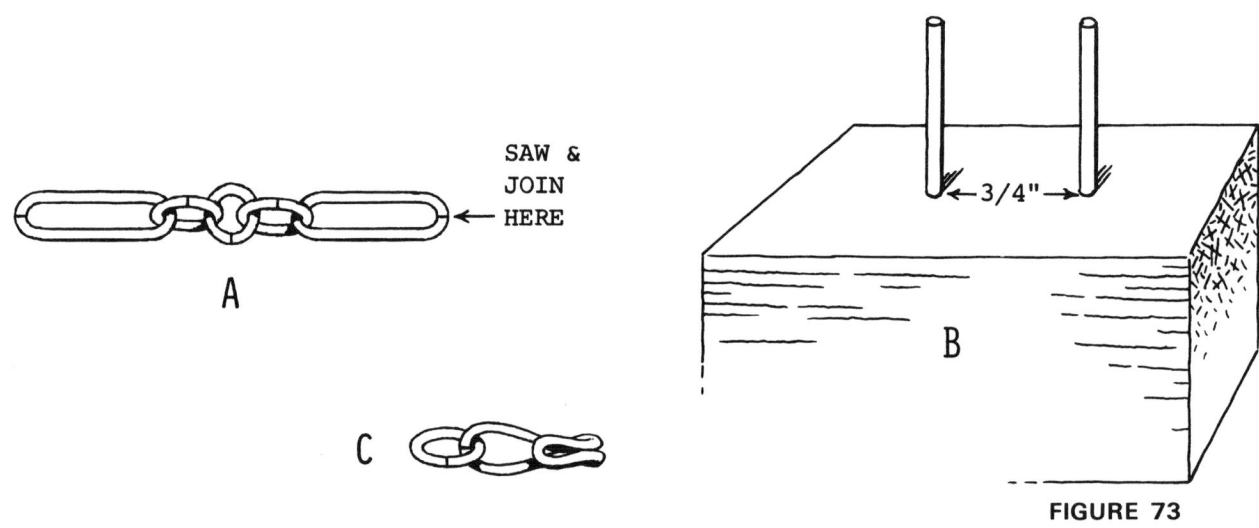

FIGURE 73

CHAIN MAKING

coiled around the nails starting at the bottom and working up. The coil is removed from the nails when the latter cannot hold any more windings. It is then sawed and soldered as shown in *A*, Fig. 73.

The hook (see *C*, Fig. 73) used on one end of the chain to secure the chain on the wearer is fashioned from an elliptical link. The link is squeezed together in the center with the long-nosed pliers, and one end is then curved back on itself with the round-nosed pliers. The hook fits into a round link on the chain's other end. The commercially made spring ring or sister hook may be used in place of the hook.

PROJECT 21: Handmade Chain, with Variations

The two chains to be described here are variations of the chain in Project 20. In the first variation the elliptical link is twisted once with pliers as shown in *A*, Fig. 74. The links are made on nails driven into a block of wood as before, then cut apart, soldered individually and twisted. The size of the nails can vary, as can the distance between them, all based on your requirements. The twisted links may be separated by one round link or two (shown in the illustration), or more, again depending on your desires.

In the second variation the links are made individually on nails driven in a block of wood as before (refer to Fig. 73). *B* in Fig. 74 shows how the link is started; *C* indicates how the free end of the wire is brought over and then—by removing the partially made link from the nails—coiled over the other free end and back over the place where the wire crosses itself.

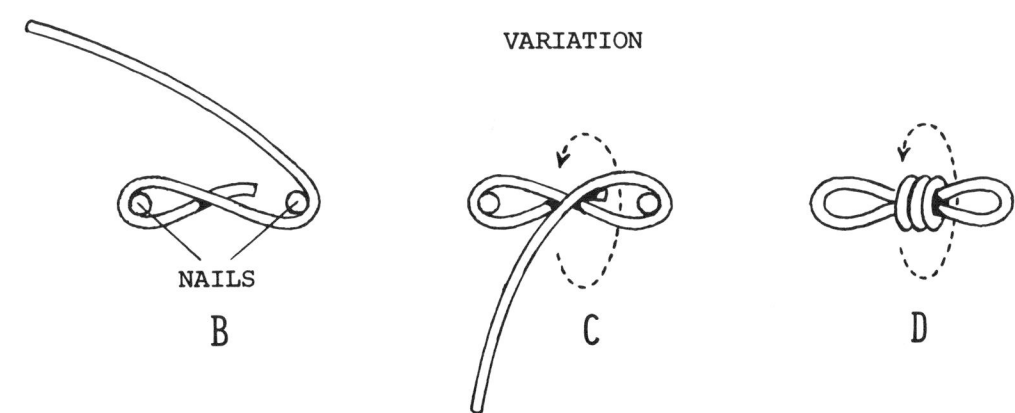

FIGURE 74

There should be at least three coils, or turns, as shown in *D*. The coil should end in the back of the link where it will not be seen. Tighten the coil with your flat-nosed pliers. These links may be connected with one or more round links as required.

Although making these coiled links takes time because they must be individually made, they do not require soldering, which, in turn, saves time. Coiling the wire tightly hardens it enough to hold the ends in place and the link together.

FIGURE 75

10/PENDANTS

A pendant may be as elaborate as one can make it without violating good taste or good design principles, or it may be as simple as suspending a set stone on a chain (Fig. 75). Many pin and brooch designs will look well as pendants and vice versa. In fact, many pins and pendants can be made to be worn either way if a joint, catch and pin stem are soldered on the back plus a device for suspending the article from a chain. Such a device must be set in back where it cannot be seen. The chain must be removable and not fixed to the pendant.

PROJECT 22: Brass Heart Pendant

This pendant is a novelty item that will probably appeal more to the younger set. The outline of the heart to be cut out is shown in A, Fig. 76. The dashed lines indicate where the item is to be cut into three parts once the drilling, piercing, filing and smoothing are accomplished. The drilling and piercing of the interior design is a matter of personal choice. You may follow the pattern shown or use your imagination.

The blackened circles indicate holes drilled for links made ¼-in. inside diameter. Do not insert the links until after the heart is cut apart. After they are in place (see B, Fig. 76), the link seams should be soldered in the usual manner. The heart is best cut apart with the metal shears, since a straighter cut can be achieved with this tool than with the jeweler's saw. If the metal curls, flatten it with your mallet.

One end of the chain that you made in Project 20 is attached to the link or jump ring labeled X, the other to that labeled Y. The catch for the chain was illustrated and explained in the same project. The three parts of the heart will move when the wearer moves, which

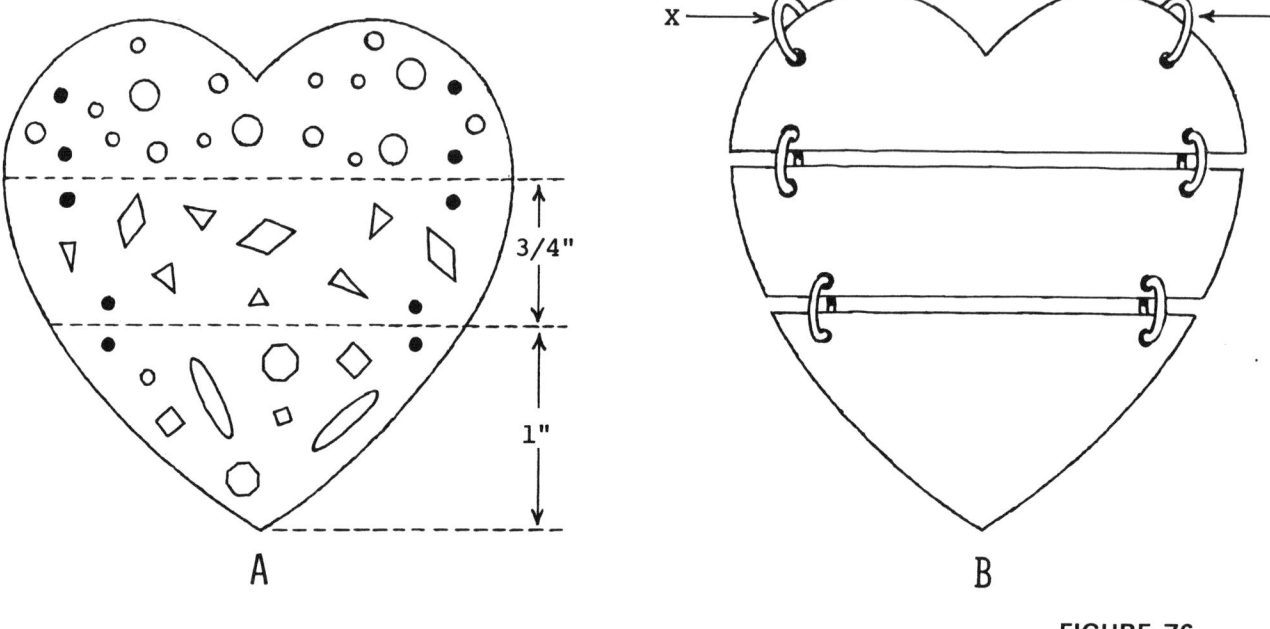

FIGURE 76

lends interest and variety to the jewelry and which is why it was made this way rather than as one solid piece.

PROJECT 23: Brass Pendant with Gemstone

This project is included so as to acquaint you with one method for setting an odd-shaped (baroque) tumbled stone, not only in a pendant but in a pin and even in earrings. You very probably will not be able to duplicate this particular pendant (shown centered in Fig. 75) because tumbled stones are usually one-of-a-kind, and it is practically impossible to find two that match perfectly. The stone used here happens to be an agate that is flat on both its large surfaces. To work in the method under discussion, the stone you select must be perfectly flat on at least one broad surface. *A*, in Fig. 77, shows the backing or plate (20-ga. brass) for the pendant. The size and shape of the stone used here is shown in *B*. You will have to design your own plate based on the stone you use.

The *X*'s in *A* indicate the part of the backing that is pierced out leaving prongs, labeled *P*, for the stone. These prongs should be located where, in your judgment, they will grip the stone securely when they are bent over. They can be made longer to accommodate a stone that is flat on one surface but which rises to a sort of sloping hill on the other. The built-in device for suspending the pendant from a chain is labeled *Y* (see *A*, Fig. 77). *C* shows the

PENDANTS

prongs bent back with the round-nosed pliers. When you have done this, check to see if the stone fits flat against the back plate and comfortably inside the prongs. Do not force the stone between the prongs since that may chip or crack it. If more room is needed, cut and bend the prongs back until the stone sits easily within them. The stone is finally set, however, only after all the other work is done.

D shows the 16-ga. brass wire that is bent to an erratic shape and soldered to the plate with Easy-grade solder. It is shaded in the sketch for clarity. The length and shape of this wire will depend on the shape and size of your pendant's plate. After the wire is soldered in place, flatten it slightly with the embossing hammer. The blackened circles represent brass beads soldered in place. The size, number and placement of these beads will also depend on the plate you have designed for your stone.

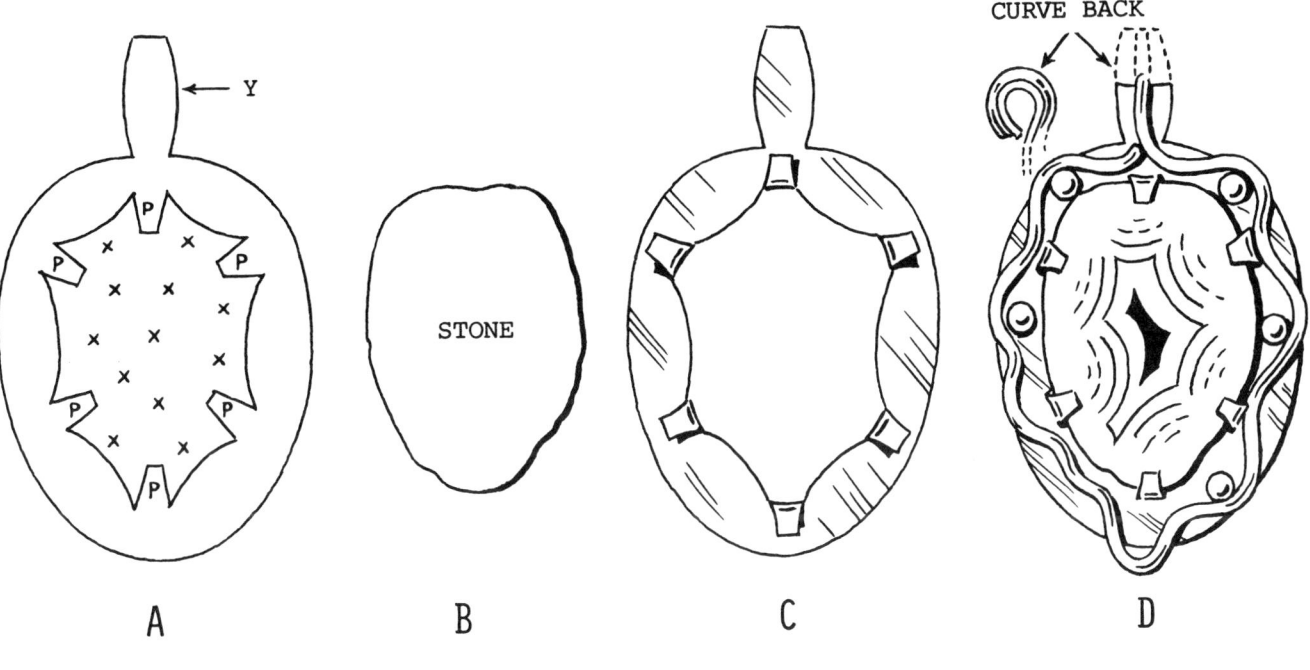

FIGURE 77

The part labeled *Y* is curved back as shown in *D*. In the author's pendant, a brass jump ring, ⅜ in. diameter, is inserted in this device. Two more rings are inserted in the first ring. These two rings each connect to a round link of the first chain made in Project 21 to suspend the pendant from the chain. The stone is set by carefully pushing and curving the prongs over it with the stone pusher and burnisher. Coloring the part of the back plate between the curved wire and the stone with antimony trichloride serves to enhance the pendant's appearance.

PROJECT 24: Silver Pendant

This book would not be complete without a silver pendant. The one illustrated here, cut from 20-ga. metal, is quite simple to make and is very attractive in appearance when completed. Transfer the design shown in *A*, Fig. 78, then cut out the outline of the piece. The small sections that are marked with *X*'s are pierced out. The lobes that protrude from the center of the article are dapped out from the underside, first with the No. 26 dapping punch and then with the No. 23. *B* shows the oval disks needed, and the dashed-line oval in *C* indicates where this disk is soldered on in the back with Easy-grade solder. Its purpose is to permit the pierced sections to be antiqued; an operation which adds to the general attractiveness of the pendant. Where the disk extends into the lower curves of the lobes, it should be filed away with the round needle file as indicated in *C*.

The pendant, of course, requires an accessory to permit it to be suspended on a chain. As shown in *D,* this can be made of 18-ga. wire or a piece of 20-ga. sheet. The letter *Y* shows approximately where the accessory should be soldered. The chain shown with this pendant was commercially made.

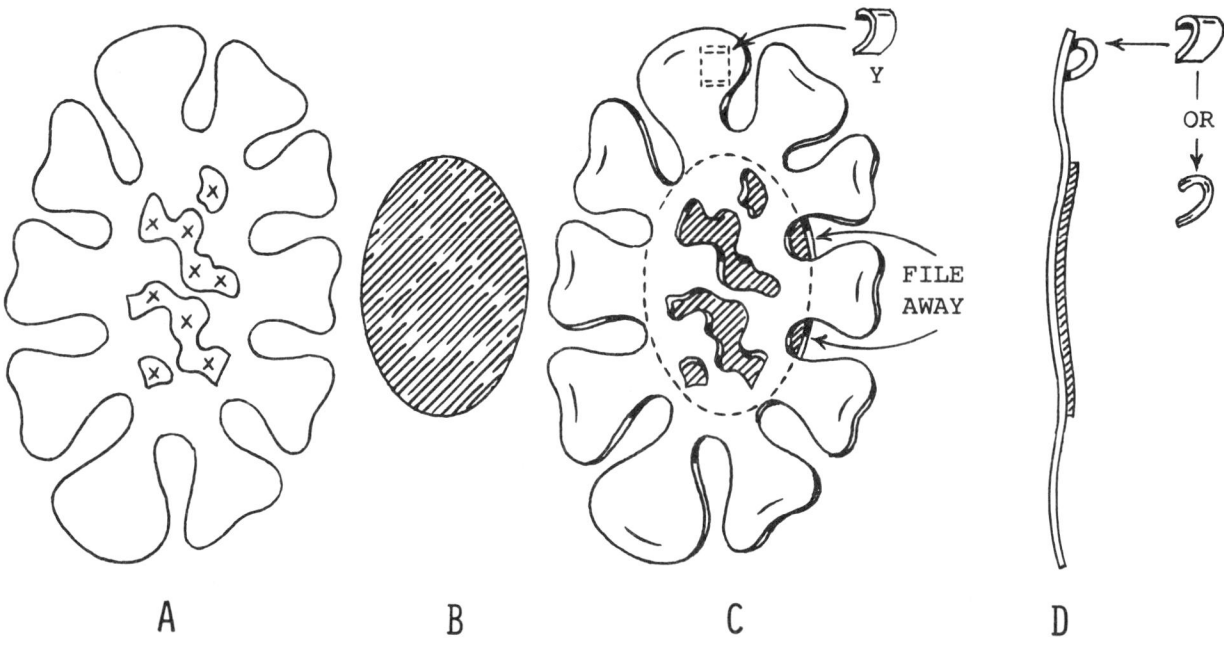

FIGURE 78

11/DESIGNING JEWELRY

You should now have reached the stage in your development as a beginning jewelry craftsman where you can stop being a strict copier of other people's work and can start developing your own ideas. Perhaps you have already made tentative efforts in that direction. If you have, or if you feel you are ready to do so, then this book has fulfilled its primary purpose.

Do not say that you have no ideas for designs. Design ideas exist everywhere. Nature alone provides an endless variety of forms that can be adapted to jewelry designs. Animals, plants, the parts of plants—seeds, pods, flowers, buds, leaves and so on—all lend themselves to such designs once they have been filtered through your imagination. Also around are manmade objects, geometric figures and other shapes that offer an endless variety of abstract and free-form possibilities. It is said that beauty lies in the eye of the beholder. One of the most important attributes of the accomplished jewelry craftsman is his ability to look at something and be able to see in his *mind's eye* how that something may be adapted to an article of jewelry.

Having a sketch pad handy on which you can doodle or rough-in ideas is a good way of developing your design capabilities. A piece of tracing paper placed over a sketch or on part of a rough drawing may enable you to trace out something that will be the design for a piece of jewelry. You should read books on the principles of good design; for, even though they usually deal in generalities, you should have some idea of what good design principles are. Visit museums, galleries and craft shows where jewelry is to be exhibited. Visit jewelry stores at every opportunity—particularly those that offer the contemporary in addition to the old, conventional, diamond-encrusted kind. In this way, you may be able to conjure up some valuable ideas of your own based on what you have seen.

Obviously there are a number of other books on jewelry making besides this one. You should get several of them from your library or even buy them, if necessary, now that you have reached this stage in your development as a maker of jewelry. These books show many fine pieces of jewelry and you may well be tempted to reproduce several of them. At this juncture, however, you should avoid the temptation. Instead, you should look at the jewelry pieces that appeal to you with the object of finding ways for adapting what you see to an article that is the product of your own ingenuity and initiative.

This is not to deny that it is extremely difficult to come up with jewelry ideas—or any ideas for that matter—that are totally original. But, again, do not interpret this to mean that you should not keep looking for original concepts. On the contrary, you should—*always!* Meanwhile you should keep working at the craft—improving your skills, perfecting your techniques, while continually learning new ones. Many times this may involve adapting items made by another to which you add something of your own. For example, take the fish pin you made in Project 18. It is primarily made from sheet silver. Look at it. Can you see the same fish, or a similar fish, constructed entirely of wire? It can be. It may even look better in wire than it does in sheet silver. This is the kind of approach that will remove the stigma of plagiarism, for you will have given each piece of jewelry a dimension of your own.

APPENDIX A

SUPPLIERS

GENERAL

AKG & Company
1114 Greentree Road
Newark, Delaware   19711

Allcraft Tool & Supply Company, Inc.
215 Park Avenue
Hicksville, New York   11801

Allcraft Tool & Supply Company, Inc.
22 West 48 Street
New York, New York   10036

Alpha Faceting Supply
Box 2133
Bremerton, Washington   98301

Anchor Tool and Supply Company, Inc.
12 John Street
New York, New York   10038

Bourget Bros.
1247 Washington Boulevard
Culver City, California   90066

Bourget Bros.
1011 Olympic Boulevard
Santa Monica, California   90404

Calsco Casting & Lapidary Supply Co.
2084 East Foothill Boulevard
Pasadena, California   91107

The Craftool Company
Wood-Ridge, New Jersey   07075

William Dixon Incorporated
Carlstadt, New Jersey   07072

SUPPLIERS

Five M Gems & Lapidary
270 East 17th Street
Costa Mesa, California 92627

The Foredom Electric Company
Bethel, Connecticut 06801

Gemex Company
Corner Hwy 395 & 76
Pala, California 92059

Grieger's Inc.
1633 East Walnut Street
Pasadena, California 91109

T. B. Hagstoz & Son
709 Sansom Street
Philadelphia, Pennsylvania 19106

C. R. Hill Company
35 West Grand River Avenue
Detroit, Michigan 48226

Lapidabrade, Inc.
8 East Eagle Road
Havertown, Pennsylvania 19803

Maroon Belle Industries, Inc.
3400 Tejon Street
Denver, Colorado 80211

Montana Assay Office
610 Southwest 2nd Avenue
Portland, Oregon 97204

Obriens
1116 North Wilcox Avenue
Hollywood, California 90038

C. W. Somers & Co.
387 Washington Street
Boston, Massachusetts

Southwest Smelting and Refining Co., Inc.
118 Broadway
P. O. Box 1298
San Antonio, Texas 78206

Southwest Smelting and Refining Co., Inc.
1712 Jackson Street
P. O. Box 2010
Dallas, Texas 75221

Technical Specialties International, Inc.
422—1st Avenue West
Seattle, Washington 98119

Tyes Rock Shop
2308 North Main Street
Dayton, Ohio 45405

Weidinger, Inc.
P. O. Box 39
Matteson, Illinois 60443

GEMSTONES ONLY

Francis Hoover
Box 4082
12445 Chandler Boulevard
North Hollywood, California 91607

International Import Company
P. O. Box 747
Stone Mountain, Georgia 30083

Lapidary International, Inc.
1228 South Beach Boulevard
Anaheim, California 92804

APPENDIX B

OTHER TOOLS AND EQUIPMENT

The tools and equipment on the following list are not mandatory, but they are nice to have because they make certain jewelry-making tasks easier, more efficient and more effective. You will have to consult jewelry catalogs for a description of each item and its purpose since our limited space does not permit an expanded treatment here.

Motor for Polishing—with tapered spindle (single shaft motor) or spindles (double shaft motor), 4-in. muslin buff for tripoli compound, 4-in. flannel buff for jeweler's rouge, 3-in. felt ring buff, 3-in. felt wheel.
Half-Round Pliers.
Mounted Tweezers—a third hand
Three Square, Square, Hand and Round Files—cuts No. 1 and No. 3 OR No. 2 and No. 4.
Needle Files—additional shapes based on what you feel you need and can use.
Riffle Files—some shapes are almost a necessity; you are the judge as to what you think you can use.
Pin Vise.
Coiled Asbestos.
Emery Cloth or Paper inside Ring Buffs—cloth preferred; for use on motor.

Steel Bristle Brush—2 in., 4 row, for imparting a satin finish to a piece of jewelry or part thereof.

Combination Drawplate and Drawtongs.

Rivet Hammer—watchmaker's type.

Flexible Shaft Machine—plus those accessories which you believe you can use to advantage based on your experience to date.

INDEX

alloy, 15
American Indian silver, 17
annealing, 65
antimony trichloride, *see* butter of antimony
antiquing, 73
appliqué, metal, 79

baroque gemstones, mounting of, 114–115
base plate, making, 90–91
beads:
    making from wire, 81, 90, 93
    making from scrap metal, 81, 89
    soldering, 81–82
bearings, making gemstone, 92
beeswax, 36
bench pin, 34
bezels:
    description of, 20–21
    making, 90–92
    measuring, 90
blemishes, removing, 71
brass, 16
brooch, placement of joint, safety catch and pin stem on, 105–108
bumping, 108

burnishing, 47, 71
burrs, elimination of, 53
butter of antimony, 73

carat, 17, 30. *Also see* karat
chainmaking, 109–112
charcoal block, preparation of, 44
chasing, 60–63
coin silver, 17
clamping metal, for drilling, 52–53
cleaning metal, 72, 77
coloring metal, 73
copper, description of, 16
cutting metal:
    angles, 56
    with jeweler's saw, 55
    with shears, 53–54

dapping, 63–64
designs:
    scribing, 52
    transferring, 51–52, 76
doming, 63
drilling metal, 52–53
drills, 36–37

INDEX

ductility, 16

ear clips, soldering, 88–89
ear wires, soldering, 86
embossing, see texturing

files, 46
  cleaning, 60
  fitting a tang, 46
filing, 58–60
  with jeweler's saw, 58
findings, definition of, 24
  kinds of, 25–28
fire scale:
  prevention, 65
  removal, 72
Florentine finish, making pseudo, 97–98
flux, use of, 24

gauging:
  sheet metal, 19
  wire, 20
gemstone setting:
  in bezel, 90–92
  with prongs, 114–115
gemstones, description of, 29–30
German silver, 16
gilding metal, 16
gold, description of, 17–18
graver liner, 97

heating frame, how to make, 44
hollow scraper, 60
hook, making, 111

jeweler's rouge, 48, 72
jeweler's saw:
  blades, 36
  cutting angles, 56
  cutting metal, 55
  description of, 36
  filing, 58–60
  inserting blade, 54
  use of, 55–57
join:
  method of soldering, 66–70
  placement of, 88
jump rings: 88, 90

karat, definition of, 17–18. *Also see* carat

lacquering, 77–78
letter styles, where to find, 102
links, making of, 109–112
liver of sulfur, 46, 73

malleability, 15
mandrels, 41–42
metal:
  annealing, 65
  chasing, 60–63
  cleaning, 72, 77
  coloring, 73
  cutting, 55
  drilling, 52–53
  piercing, 57–58
  polishing, 72, 77
  smoothing, 71, 76
metal appliqué, 79
metal dust and scrap, salvaging of, 31–32
Mexican silver, 17

nickel silver, 16

oxidation, 16, 24

pickling, 45, 66
piercing metal, 57–58
pin stem, sizing, 27, 107–108
platinum, description of, 18
polishing metal, 72, 77
polishing brush, making, 48
potassium sulfide, *see* liver of sulfur

INDEX

pusher:
   how to make, 70
   use of, 70

removing blemishes, 71
repoussé, 64
ring:
   making a shank from wire, 102–103
   pattern making, 99–100
   sizing, 42, 99
ring clamp, 34
ring shank, making, 102–103
riveting:
   pin stems, 107–108

safety catch:
   placement of, 105–107
   soldering, 106–107
Scotch stone, use of, 47
scrap metal, making beads from, 81
   salvaging, 31–32
scribing design, 52
shears, metal, 34–35
   using, 53–54
silver, description of, 17
smoothing metal, 71, 76

solder:
   flux, 24, 69
   grades, 22–23
   preparation of, 67
soldering, 66–67
   hard, 68–70
   soft, 67
   use of yellow ochre in, 45, 70
sterling silver, 17
stone pusher, 92
sweat soldering, 95

texturing, 75
thrumming, 58
tie bar, bending and forming, 96
transferring designs, 51–52, 76
Tripoli compound, 48, 72
troy weight, 20

vise:
   padding jaws, 33

wire, making beads from, 81
wire twisting, 82–84
workbench, 31–32

yellow ochre, use of, 45, 70

5613